A History of Quebec Nationalism

Gilles Gougeon
Translated by Louisa Blair, Robert Chodos and Jane Ubertino

James Lorimer & Company, Publishers
Toronto, 1994

DB# 119 74 14

Originally published as *Histoire du nationalisme québécois: Entrevues avec sept spécialistes.*

Copyright ©1993 VLB Éditeur and Société Radio-Canada
Copyright ©1994 Translation by Louisa Blair, Robert Chodos and Jane Ubertino

James Lorimer & Company Ltd. acknowledges with thanks the support of the Canada Council, the Ontario Arts Council and the Ontario Publishing Centre in the development of writing and publishing in Canada.

Canadian Cataloguing in Publication Data

A History of Quebec nationalism

Translation of: Histoire du nationalisme québécois.
ISBN 1-55028-441-X (bound) ISBN 1-55028-440-1 (pbk.)

1. Quebec (Province) - History - Autonomy and independence movement - Miscellanea. 2. Nationalism - Quebec (Province) - History - Miscellanea. I. Gougeon, Gilles.

FC2920.N38H5713 1994   971.4   C94-930917-6
F1052.95.N38H5713 1994

*Fc
2920
.N4
H5713
1994*

James Lorimer & Company Ltd., Publishers
35 Britain Street
Toronto, Ontario M5A 1R7

Printed and bound in Canada

Contents

Preface

This book had its origin in a series of programs broadcast on the CBC French network on January 21, 22, 23 and 24, 1992. Journalist Gilles Gougeon and producer Pierre Devrœde first presented "A History of Quebec Nationalism" as part of the nightly public affairs program Le Point.

This series, the fruit of painstaking archival research, was unique in the history of Canadian television. It took the form of evidence given by seven specialists in the field of Quebec and Canadian history. VLB Éditeur, the publisher of the original French edition of this book, wanted to make the transcripts of these academics' remarks available to the public. In explaining the development of Quebec nationalism and putting it in context, they come as close as anyone has to a consensus of the work of the many historians who have studied this question for decades.

However, this book is not the result of a collective effort by the scholars who were interviewed. They responded individually to Gougeon's questions and in no way participated in the editing of this book. The opinions expressed in these pages or in any other publications are those of the scholars themselves.

As the history of nationalism makes clear, Quebec has become an open, pluralistic and tolerant society where the free exchange of ideas is a basic fact of daily life. The scholars interviewed in this book don't all analyse the facts that they relate in the same way or draw the same conclusions. In other publications, some have even expressed diametrically opposed opinions on the interpretation of our history and the political options that might follow. We think the material presented here is free from these opinions and political stands. The scholars have played by the rules, staying with the facts and putting them into context.

It took courage for Gougeon and Devrœde to tackle the theme of nationalism on public television when this issue raises so much controversy and debate, as recent political events have made clear. Our goal here is to follow up their initiative by publishing in full the remarks that were broadcast in this series so as to help us better understand the whys and wherefores of Quebecers' assertion of their national identity.

VLB Éditeur

Introduction

September 1991. I have to go to Samarkand, in Uzbekistan. After the failed coup against Gorbachev, the producers of *Le Point* are dispatching me to the Soviet Union to put together a series of televised reports on the emergence of democracy in the old empire of the Czars.

On September 5, I land in Uzbekistan, 3,500 kilometres southeast of Moscow, to determine whether or not the new Soviet revolution has spread beyond Russia. Far from Moscow, I have heard, the wellspring of democracy is being drowned out by nationalism. On my arrival in Samarkand, I secretly make contact with a colleague on whom I'm counting for an explanation of the local sociopolitical dynamic. "He'll be able to give you a sense of the situation," I'm told. "It's a fight for power among the Uzbeks, the Tajiks and the Russians within an Asian culture and in an Islamic context."

First meeting. Alexander is waiting for me on a park bench. He gets up, shakes my hand, introduces himself and says something that I take to be a formality. The interpreter, taken aback, translates it for me: "So, is Quebec going to separate?"

More than 10,000 kilometres from Quebec, in a city that was on the legendary silk route and has known Tamerlane, Genghis Khan and Alexander the Great, this man brought me back home with a jolt. In Samarkand I was being asked the same question that hundreds of people have asked me over the course of my reporting in Africa, Latin America, central Europe, Scandinavia, the Persian Gulf, western Europe, the United States, Canada and Quebec.

On my return to Montreal in mid-September, I was barely in the office before the producers of *Le Point* summoned me and informed me that I had to get to work immediately on a subject that was large, complex and explosive, but fascinating: the history of nationalism in French Canada. I have never looked back.

I will admit, though, that for several seconds I had the impression that my bosses had just opened the porthole of a moving rocket and I had been sucked out through it, with no oxygen or parachute, into the interstellar space of the past. How could I tell this story on television, in the time allotted to me and in the setting of a nightly public affairs program? How was I going to sustain the interest of

television viewers who are used to the strong emotions of a block-
buster miniseries? What period would I cover? What *was* French
Canada, anyway? What was nationalism? These were some of the
questions that added to the dizzy spell brought on by this monumen-
tal assignment. All the more so in that, although I have a passion for
history, I am a generalist who had always described myself as specializing in knowing nothing.

Then I thought of my colleague Alexander in Samarkand. I
thought to myself that I had to be able to make *him* understand the
history of French Canadian and Quebec nationalism. If, by the end
of this, I could make a man in Samarkand understand this history,
surely I could interest my fellow citizens. Thus began one of the most
wonderful journeys in my whole career as a reporter.

A First-rate Team

I made this journey in the company of producer Pierre Devrœde and
his assistant Jean-Claude Beauséjour. From the outset we needed a
guide, as we didn't want to make a trip into the past without the help
of an expert. We chose Richard Desrosiers, professor of history at
the University of Quebec at Montreal (UQAM), whom everyone
spoke of as a great teacher with a good grasp of history. We were
not disappointed.

We decided that we would try to present material that came as
close as possible to being generally agreed on by historians. Obviously there is no such thing as an "official history," a single and
definitive interpretation of the facts, except in countries with totali-
tarian regimes. However, we had to tell the story in such a way that
most historians would easily recognize it.

We then fixed the time period we would cover. When did a
national identity start to emerge? From all the evidence, it seemed
we needed to go back to the French regime, to New France, to the
time when the first generation born in Canada started to differentiate
themselves from their parents who still considered themselves
French. So our trip was to take us from the final years of French rule
— from about 1740, twenty years before the defeat and the handing
over of the French colony to England — right up to 1991.

In our account of the events of recent years, it would be impossible
to lay claim to the rigorous detachment that historians demand. So
we realized we had to specify that we were not historians but journalists. History would be our main subject, and historians would be

our witnesses, but the final result would be a presentation by journalists looking with curiosity through a rear-view mirror, aiming to help our television audience and our readers better understand the development of nationalism.

After determining how we would divide this history into major periods, we asked Richard Desrosiers to help us find the leading experts in each of these periods, taking into account not just their competence but also their ability to present their part of the story in an engaging manner. Above all we had to produce a good TV show.

And this is how seven distinguished scholars came to accompany us on our long search for national identity and the assertion of French Canadian nationhood:

Robert Lahaise (history department, UQAM): from the latter years of New France to the Constitutional Act of 1791.

Jean-Paul Bernard (history department, UQAM): from the Patriotes in the early nineteenth century to the Act of Union of 1840.

Réal Bélanger (history department, Laval University): from Confederation in 1867 to 1917 (Louis Riel, the Boer War and the conscription crisis of 1917).

Pierre Trépanier (history department, University of Montreal): nationalism during the time of Lionel Groulx.

Richard Desrosiers (history department, UQAM): 1930 to 1960 (Maurice Duplessis, the conscription plebiscite, the Quiet Revolution).

Robert Comeau (history department, UQAM): fascism in the 1930s, the politician Georges-Émile Lapalme, the historian Maurice Séguin.

Louis Balthazar (political science department, Laval University): nationalism today.

Each of these people agreed to meet with me for a few hours for a pre-interview, without the cameras rolling. I thus had the privilege of a "private lesson" of a sort that few students have ever experienced. It was fascinating. After this meeting, each scholar was invited to take up once again — on camera this time — the remarks and comments he and I had prepared together. It is the outcome of these interviews that is presented here.

Each interview lasted between an hour and an hour and a half. In addition to providing us with on-air material, the interviews helped us draft the script of the TV series. That is how the brilliant idea of publishing the complete version of these interviews came to us. It would have been senseless to leave these timely remarks, syntheses and comments to gather dust in our archives. Moreover, hadn't we achieved something that would have been very difficult without the magic of television — bringing together seven of the foremost scholars on the subject of nationalism?

Why This Series, Now?

The context for the decision to produce and broadcast this television series at this precise point in the history of Quebec — January 21-24, 1992 — was the upcoming referendum on redefining the relationship between Quebec and the rest of Canada, which was to take place sometime in 1992. This was also the post–Meech Lake period — the Allaire Report, the Bélanger-Campeau and Beaudoin-Dobbie commissions. Both Quebec and Canada were once again asking questions about the future. The word *nationalism* was being alternately trampled on, trumpeted and booed. Some people were concentrating their efforts on re-establishing the link made in the thirties between nationalism and fascism, nationalism and racism, nationalism and intolerance. Others simply saw in nationalism the popular expression of a unique national identity.

We therefore chose to use the medium of television, with all its strengths and weaknesses, to show how this national identity had developed: from French to *Canadien* to French Canadian to Québécois. We have tried to understand the people and the events that marked this evolution from an ethnic nationalism to a linguistic and territorial one.

I would like to thank the academics who helped us; producer Pierre Devrœde and his assistant Jean-Claude Beauséjour; the staffs of the CBC's archives and its music department; the museums, research centres and companies that allowed us access to their archives; the senior producers of *Le Point* (Jean-Marc Desjardins, François Brunet and Alain Saulnier); and the management of VLB Éditeur, which took the initiative to publish the complete text of the interviews.

I have always thought that a television program should encourage people to go off and read more and become better informed on the subject presented. This book enables people to do just that, and is thus a natural follow-up to the series televised in January 1992.

Gilles Gougeon
Journalist
CBC

Part One

The first program begins the study of nationalism, covering the period between the end of the French regime and the defeat of 1759 to Confederation in 1867. In it we see how, from the beginning, people here considered themselves different from the French, the British and the Americans. Placed in a minority position in their own country, the *"Canadiens"* — that is, the Francophones — made deals with the "English," with whom they sought ways of building a democratic country.

The historians interviewed are Robert Lahaise and Jean-Paul Bernard.

Interview with Robert Lahaise

Gilles Gougeon: Mr. Lahaise, first of all I'd like to discuss what it means to be "Canadien." At what point did the inhabitants of this country start to think of themselves as "les Canadiens"?

Robert Lahaise: I want to look at this question in a couple of ways — and it's a huge question. One way is to look at its geographical aspect and the other is to look at the evolution of the word *Canadien*.

Let's start with geography. Under French rule, New France was an immense territory covering the whole area from what is now the Maritimes in the east to the Rockies in the west, and from Hudson Bay in the north to the Gulf of Mexico in the south, except for the thirteen American colonies located between the Atlantic coast and the Appalachians. There were seven regions in New France — Acadia, Louisiana and others — but the real heart of New France was Canada, stretching from Vaudreuil to Les Éboulements along the north shore of the St. Lawrence, and from Châteauguay to Rimouski along the south shore. In fact by the time French rule ended, 70,000 out of the 100,000 people in New France lived in Canada. This is why you often hear people talk misleadingly about "New France, or Canada."

Let's move on from the geography to the word, Canada. The name dates back to 1535, Jacques Cartier's second voyage. He sailed up the St. Lawrence — although of course it wasn't called that yet — and on August 10, the Feast of St. Lawrence, he arrived at a bay that he named after the saint. Mercator, the famous sixteenth-century Dutch geographer, later extended this name to the entire St. Lawrence River, but as far as Cartier was concerned, this was the Canada River. Why Canada? Because when Cartier made his way up the river, there were three "kingdoms," as he called them. The first, which he named the Kingdom of the Saguenay, appeared to him to be a mysterious, alluring place where untold riches hinted at by the Iroquois would be found. Then there was the Kingdom of Canada, stretching a dozen miles upstream and downstream from what we now know as Quebec City. So "Canada," in fact, signified a town, a collection of longhouses where a settled people were living in dwellings about a hundred feet long by thirty feet wide.

Gilles Gougeon: So it's a Native American word.

Robert Lahaise: Yes. The capital was Stadacona, an Iroquoian word meaning a promontory or a rock. Later on it would be known as Quebec, an Algonkian word meaning "a narrowing of the river."

The second kingdom was Canada. And the third, Hochelaga, now Montreal, means "beaver dam" in Iroquoian. When Cartier spoke of "Canadiens" in 1535, he was referring to the Iroquois he had met there. When Lescarbot wrote his history of New France, which was published in Paris in 1609, he was still writing of "Canadiens," but he didn't just mean the inhabitants of Canada in Quebec, he meant the entire population of the St. Lawrence Valley.

Gilles Gougeon: Did that include the settlers from France?

Robert Lahaise: There weren't any. A handful had come with Cartier and Roberval between 1534 and 1543, but all either had left again or had died. There was no French settlement in Quebec until 1608, when about thirty people wintered there. It was a disaster, mostly because of scurvy. In 1609, the Algonquins came and asked the eight survivors if they would join them in their war against the Iroquois. Champlain had no choice, especially since there were more than 100,000 Algonquins and they were close neighbours, while there were fewer than 20,000 Iroquois and they lived some 400 kilometres away. To get back to your question, there were no *Canadiens*, as we understand the word, born in Canada yet. But there were Native peoples, who were often designated as *Canadiens* in the correspondence of the day.

The word *Canadiens,* in the sense of people born here of French parents, began to appear during Frontenac's first tour of duty as governor, between 1672 and 1682. When a friend of his, Baron de La Hontan, wrote on the subject he spoke of settlers interchangeably as "creole" or "canadien." But by the early eighteenth century, *Canadiens* had clearly begun to prevail and would remain dominant until about 1800: "les Canadiens" were Francophones who lived in the St. Lawrence Valley. But in the meantime the Loyalists, fleeing the newly independent United States, came to settle here. And as there were now two distinct nations, we soon began calling ourselves French Canadians. This term stuck until the Quiet Revolution in the 1960s, when we reaffirmed our identity by rejecting the term *French Canadian* and calling ourselves *"Québécois."*

Gilles Gougeon: How does the geographical Canada fit into this?

Robert Lahaise: In 1760, we were defeated. By the way, I've never been able to understand why we insist on calling it a "conquest"! But we'll return later to the question of the "glorious defeat."

At the time of the defeat, Canada consisted of the St. Lawrence Valley region that I've been talking about. King George III's Royal Proclamation of 1763 turned what had been Canada into the colony of Quebec, which reached from the Ottawa to the St. John River and which included the Gaspé. This was in fact the area inhabited by the "Canadiens."

In the following years, the thirteen American colonies revolted against their motherland. So that we wouldn't be tempted to become their allies, we were granted the Quebec Act of 1774, which restored a large portion of our rights that had been suspended or lost in 1760 — such as religion, language and law — as well as the territory of Labrador and a chunk that stretched from the Great Lakes to the Ohio. It was called the Province of Quebec, and it stayed that way until 1791, when the word Canada appeared on the scene again.

Although we're just looking at geography, let me point out that, in 1791, with the coexistence between French and English speakers by now fairly well established, England decided to grant us the Constitutional Act. This created Upper Canada (the future Ontario) for the Anglophones, and Lower Canada (our future Province of Quebec), principally for the Francophones.

Then came the 1837-38 rebellions and the British backlash, which saw the two become a single colony known as the Province of Canada. This led a pretty shaky existence until 1867, when Confederation gathered the four provinces of Quebec, Ontario, New Brunswick and Nova Scotia into one dominion, called Canada. To cut a long story short, six more provinces were added between 1870 and 1949, and so we have Canada as it is now.

Newfoundland was the last to join in 1949, and so some say that it was really John Cabot who discovered Canada, when he discovered Newfoundland in 1497, rather than Jacques Cartier in 1534. But it's a false argument: Native people had already lived here for 30,000 years. They're the real discoverers.

To conclude our discussion on geographical Canada, suffice it to say that it now extends from the Atlantic to the Pacific, and from the 49th Parallel to the Arctic Ocean.

Gilles Gougeon: At what point did the "Canadiens," that is, the non-Natives who were born here, start to differentiate themselves from the French who came to Canada?

Robert Lahaise: Between 1534 and 1634, there was nothing to speak of in terms of population growth. The French continued to come and go, or else die here, but in 1632 the population was still really starting from scratch. In fact the French in Quebec only numbered twenty or so. The English had seized our territory in 1629, and most of the settlers, including Champlain, had gone home to France. With the Treaty of Saint-Germain-en-Laye, France reclaimed its colony in 1632, and by the following year the population had grown to 2,500, non-Natives that is, and of this number about half were born in this country. We call this the *génération de l'enracinement* (the founding generation). For the first time we had 1,200 people — not many, I know, but it was a start — who were born here of French parents and who weren't about to jump on the boat and go home to France. These people were not French as such, which is why they had already begun to adapt and differentiate themselves.

It was largely thanks to the Native people that they adapted to the vastness of the land. Let's take for example their use of snowshoes in the winter. When Carignan's regiment arrived here in 1665, they wanted to go off and fight the Iroquois. The Canadiens told them that you don't go anywhere in winter, or at least if you must, you go on snowshoes, but it was in vain. The French chose not to listen, and their expedition was a total flop.

People were already realizing that you couldn't move around or fight wars here the same way you could in the mother country. We'll come back to this, because it's an important aspect of the differentiation. The canoe was the other thing that helped them adapt to the hugeness of the territory, and very soon they became trappers. They also found another extraordinary kind of freedom here. In France, society was highly stratified. There were three classes: the aristocracy, the clergy and the third estate. But here, and I mean nothing pejorative by this, 95 per cent of the 10,000 immigrants who arrived during French rule didn't even have the wherewithal for their passage home. Another phenomenon was that people were obviously trying to better themselves, which is quite normal for people who are economically weak — people who are mostly young and strong, but penniless. This resulted in a kind of social levelling, and not at the lowest common denominator. Does it mean anything, anyway, to be high or low on the social scale? In any case, there wasn't the social stratification here that there was in Europe. North America democratized its people as much in New France as in New England. So much so, in fact, that the French administrators repeatedly took great offence. Hocquart, one intendant, wrote in 1737 that the Canadiens were "intractable by nature." At the very moment of our defeat, Montcalm spoke of our overly independent spirit, and the Comte de Bougainville went so far as to declare "We seem to be two different nations, indeed enemies."

Gilles Gougeon: Enemies?

Robert Lahaise: Enemies, yes. The word does sound a bit strong, but if you look at what was happening in the military sphere, we certainly behaved quite differently. Frontenac, one leader who understood our ways very well, observed "Here, it's every man to his own tree." The fighting style was exactly like that of the Native people, and not at all like the kind of strategy the Europeans used, with commands like "Ready, gentlemen of England, and fire!," which required their soldiers to die dutifully one row at a time. Here, you just hoped like hell that your tree would protect you — that was one of the main differences between the Canadien militiamen and the French regulars.

In 1759, when New France made a last-ditch effort to survive, we called up 14,000 Canadien militiamen, 5,000 French regulars and 2,000 Natives. And remember that the entire population of Canada was only 70,000. At the time, our two military leaders had completely opposite notions of what the future colony would look like. Notice, too, that for the first time — and also the last! — the governor general was a true Canadien. His name was Pierre de Rigaud de Cavagnal, Marquis de Vaudreuil, and he was the son of Philippe de Rigaud, who had been governor during the first quarter of the eighteenth century.

Gilles Gougeon: So he was born here. During the conflict itself, though, what were the important differences between the French and the Canadiens?

Robert Lahaise: It was the strategy itself that was quite different. Vaudreuil, a Canadien, insisted that we should keep the whole of New France, from Hudson Bay to the Gulf of Mexico. Then the fur trade could continue and eventually lead to the development of all the other natural resources, such as fisheries and forestry. Also that way, the Canadiens, who had alliances with about twenty Indian nations, could effectively prevent the New England colonists from spreading west. Otherwise, said Vaudreuil, the Canadiens would have to hunker down in the St. Lawrence Valley and become dead-end farmers with no future to speak of, and they certainly didn't want that. So strictly speaking, the famous agricultural vocation of the Québécois has no basis in fact! But we had to eat to live, and having no more access to trade, we had to grow potatoes and carrots! Again, I'm not implying farming is a demeaning occupation; I'm simply saying we have to stop allowing ourselves to be lulled into passivity by these comforting myths.

Gilles Gougeon: And what was the attitude of the French?

Robert Lahaise: Montcalm had perhaps a more realistic attitude, which was that we simply couldn't keep all our territories. We numbered around 70,000, but there were a million and a half Americans, and, what's more, our territory surrounded theirs and prevented them from moving west. There was only one solution, which was to retreat to the St. Lawrence Valley, where perhaps we could manage to coexist peacefully with the Anglophones around us.

Gilles Gougeon: But during the battle of the Plains, for example?

Robert Lahaise: At the famous battle of the Plains of Abraham on the night of September 12, 1759, 4,800 English soldiers scaled the cliffs at Anse-au-Foulon and silently overcame the guards that they encountered. A somewhat brutal awakening for the French, to be faced with these troops. Montcalm himself commanded 4,000 men, so there were 4,000 ranged against 4,800 — which shouldn't necessarily make a tragic difference. Some people have said that if Montcalm had waited for Bougainville's troops, he could have had 12,000 extra men with whom to fight the English. But I think that's a mistaken interpretation of history. The English were 35,000 strong and they were all set to scale the cliffs, too. Moreover, when you come face to face with 5,000 troops in combat position, you don't linger over lofty theoretical discussions. Also, the 2,000 Canadien militiamen would leap out and start firing without waiting for orders, as they had learned to do in the woods. The 2,000 French regulars were overwhelmed by events, and the English had received very strict orders: "Wait until they're less than forty feet away before you fire."

It was a disaster. Some people treat it as a joke, pointing out that the battle lasted less than an hour. Maybe so, but in those fifty minutes some 1,200 French and Canadien soldiers and 600 British perished on the Plains. Anyway, there's really no point in discussing what strategies might have led to victory in 1759.

We were 70,000 against a million and a half, and we were blocking a population twenty times our size from advancing westward. France had decided that Canada was costing it a fortune, and England clearly had a superior fleet. Even if we hadn't been defeated in 1759 or 1760, we would have been defeated later, just as we had nearly been beaten during the Phips invasion in 1690 and the Walker invasion in 1711. England sought to control North America, while France had a short-sighted colonial policy.

Gilles Gougeon: There was a difference in the domain of military strategy, then, between the French and the Canadiens. Were there any other marked differences between the two groups?

Robert Lahaise: Yes. In the economic domain, among others. In New France there were two major commercial enterprises. The fisheries, to begin with, which brought in five or six million livres a year (a good worker could earn around two livres a day). But the trouble with the fisheries was that France didn't actually need us. Thousands of French fishermen simply left France every year to come and fish the banks off Newfoundland and the Maritimes, and then went back home to France. Thus, in 1760, France was rather more interested in Canadian fish than in the Canadiens. France signed a treaty with England that allowed it to keep the fishery in Saint-Pierre and Miquelon and on the Grand Banks of Newfoundland. So, in fact, the great fishing industry was of no benefit whatsoever to the Canadiens.

Then there was the fur trade, whose importance has probably been exaggerated. It generated transactions worth a million livres a year, quite a lot less than the value of the fisheries. Except that with the fur trade, France needed the Canadiens, and the Canadiens needed the Natives. The Natives trapped the beaver and the Canadiens went to fetch it from them. As the trade was a French monopoly, only the company that held the monopoly had the right to engage in it, so that company managed to secure three-quarters of the profits for itself. As for the remaining quarter, it went largely to the *coureurs de bois*, who were somewhat aristocratic adventurers and spent most of the money on exotic guns, fancy clothes and good wines — all imported from France!

So there was nothing in it for us as far as the fisheries were concerned, and we retained about 12 per cent of the profits from the fur trade! All that was left was the retail trade. At that time representatives of the big French companies, known as *marchands forains*, were coming over here.

Gilles Gougeon: Travelling salesmen —

Robert Lahaise: Yes, and they had an obvious advantage in that they had access to credit and their merchandise came in at wholesale prices. So we were eternally destined to run corner stores! At one point towards the end of French rule, Bigot[1] and his cronies had completely monopolized all trade and had stolen so much from us that some Canadiens were saying to themselves "Even if we're defeated, it can't be much worse than it is under Bigot!" It's all relative, however. Historian Fernand Ouellet points out that only fifteen years after our defeat, three-quarters of the economy was already in the hands of the Anglophones! But this is the sad reality of being conquered: it spelled the end of any trade other than that between England and its colonies, and we were ruined. So people started going around saying "Business is for the English, but hey, culture is for us!" And once we had got going on this tide of rationalization, we started using the word "conquest" for our defeat. Imagine the French talking about the "victory" at Waterloo. And better still, towards the end of the eighteenth century we had started calling it a "providential conquest."

There are two reasons why we grovelled to the point of saying we were happy to be conquered. The political reason was the Constitutional Act of 1791, which granted us the right to vote. Chief Justice William Smith told us that we had finally graduated from tyranny to government by Parliament. Then there was the religious reason, which was that although during the French Revolution there was violent anticlericism, in Quebec, the English left us in peace on this question through the Quebec Act. If we had continued under French rule, the clergy said, Catholicism would have been banned, whereas under the English it was permitted. And so "Hurray for the providential conquest!"

Gilles Gougeon: Summing up this question of identity, then, why is it that people here started calling themselves Canadiens even before the defeat?

Robert Lahaise: There's no question that people have been called Canadiens since Frontenac's time, or the late seventeenth century. By necessity people here had their own land, their own families and farms. Their identity was clearly emerging in their way of life, in their speech. We know that there were thirty-five provinces in France, many of them with their own local accent, indeed sometimes practically their own language. Here the accent was almost uniform, and the reason for this is our first mothers. Let me explain. At first, only men came out to the colony. But as it was meant to be an offshoot of France, between 1665 and 1673 about 900 *"filles du roi"* [2] were sent over, that is, orphans who were raised by religious sisters at the king's expense. They weren't quite the legendary "Amazons of the bedroom" that the con artist La Hontan talks about. Anyway, the *filles du roi* were sent over to balance the sexes and to procreate quickly. As they all came from the Paris region, and as most of us are their descendants, they are responsible for the uniformity of our spoken French. Since we were separated from France by 5,000 kilometres, and then were abandoned by the mother country in 1760, this developed into an accent particular to Quebec, as seems to me only natural.

Gilles Gougeon: Could we now look at another way that we identified or characterized ourselves, namely the attitude of the Canadiens towards the Americans and towards the cause of independence in the United States? Was this another area in which our stance differed? If we no longer identified with the French, did we consider ourselves North Americans?

Robert Lahaise: This is a very important point. Briefly, everyone knows about the American Revolution. But what did it have to do with us? Here's what. The Seven Years' War (1756 to 1763) had cost England very dearly, and in the aftermath of the battle, England said to its thirteen American colonies "We took New France off your hands, now you can help us pay some of our war debts." We all know what the reply to that was: *No taxation without representation.* Under this threat from the English, the Americans were looking around for future allies. Among others, the Canadiens might just fit the bill, they thought, having been beaten by the English fifteen years earlier. After all, "the enemy of my enemy is my friend."

But this would turn out to be only partially true. When the Americans invaded Canada in 1775, the Canadiens were sympathetic on the whole. But — and it's a major but — they were absolutely convinced that the Americans would be defeated. England was the great world power in 1775. There were only two million Americans and their army must surely be pitiful, because even though they were twenty times as numerous as the Canadiens, they had still needed England to beat us.

In addition, Bishop Briand threatened anyone who collaborated with the invaders, in any way, with excommunication. The clergy and the nobility, we might add, were pleased with the Quebec Act, which had just been passed, and were trying to convince the Canadiens to go back to being the proud militiamen they had been fifteen years earlier. But — and here's the rub — this time they were to fight side by side with the English! And, in fact, out of about 20,000 potential conscripts, only 800 fought on the English side, and perhaps 400 on the American side.

In 1778, France formally entered the conflict on the side of the Americans, who held out the promise that we would be saved by our erstwhile motherland. Unrest broke out again in the St. Lawrence Valley, and a priest even used the tabernacle to hide messages from "insurgents." Reality proved a lot less romantic than this flashy propaganda. After only fifteen years, history had again reduced us to our sad role as pawns. Between the fall of Montreal in 1760 and the Treaty of Paris in 1763, a number of British members of Parliament had said, "We should by no means keep Canada. Let's give it back to France instead, and then the French threat will make New England realize how much they need us as allies." In 1778, Louis XVI's France replied, "We certainly won't take Canada back, and then the English threat will make New England realize how much they need *us* as allies."

What is the moral of these dealings with the Americans? On the one hand, for the first time we had refused to obey our traditional leaders, the clergy and the nobility, and we were partaking fully in the anti-establishment spirit of the time, which could be seen both in New England and among the Encyclopedists in France. On the other hand, we were starting to vaguely realize that the great powers were only interested in us as exchange currency or as cannon fodder. We were to recall this in 1914 and again in 1939.

Gilles Gougeon: In 1791 there was the Constitutional Act, which would later give rise to stirrings of revolt, led by Papineau and his whole group. How would you place this quest for identity in the context of the Constitutional Act of 1791?

Robert Lahaise: The leaders of Quebec, at least, had very quickly been satisfied by 1774. Maurice Séguin, an important nationalist historian, said that for the first time England had given its blessing to the separateness of the French Canadian nation. But the independence of the United States, which was ratified by the Treaty of Versailles in 1783, would temper these gains. Some 90,000 Loyalists left the United States, and nearly half of them came and settled in the British colonies of North America. Some left because they were mystically convinced that they couldn't thrive without British institutions; others, having collaborated with the English, could no longer stay in the U.S.; and a certain number were suddenly overcome with love for England when they saw how generous it was towards all those who abandoned house and home to remain faithful to it. About 35,000 made for the Maritimes — there was no shortage of space there since the Acadians had all been deported — and 7,000 made for the future Ontario. Contrary to the predictions of the first two governors, Murray and Carleton (under whom we had reasonably good political status), Francophones might not always be in the majority north of the United States after all. In any case, we couldn't impose French law and the Catholic faith on the Loyalists. The situation required a new regime that would allow both Anglophone and Francophone populations to evolve naturally.

This was the Constitutional Act of 1791, dividing the colony of Quebec into two provinces: Upper Canada, where the Anglophones would be the majority, and Lower Canada, where the Francophones would be the majority. Better still, a democratic system would be established in each province, with the assumption that each majority would legislate according to its respective needs and advantages.

Another illusory promise. Up to 1791 we knew that the only rights we had depended on the good will of our governors. But from the moment our first delegates were elected to Parliament, they sincerely believed they could legislate on our behalf. Now up to 1848, the governor effectively had absolute powers. He could impose his right to veto and he had the support of the members he had named to the Legislative Council. Frustrated, the members of the Legislative Assembly soon became radicalized and formed the Parti Patriote, led by Louis-Joseph Papineau. Until 1822, Papineau sincerely believed that Lower Canada would thrive under British institutions, and that with their help it might even be heading for almost complete autonomy. In fact, he was so enthusiastic that when George III died in 1820, Papineau appointed himself eulogist, saying that this king had fortunately replaced the corruption of Louis XV and that British democracy was going to enable us to fulfil all our hopes. And he added, squaring the circle as our paradoxical leaders so often do, "Let us behave like English subjects and independent men." Just as the Statute of Westminster stipulated in 1931: a Commonwealth made up of equal countries linked by their "common allegiance to the Crown." Or better still, as we say today, "an independent Quebec in a united Canada"!

But let's not jump the gun. Let's get back to 1822, when Papineau learned that London had come within a hair's breadth of quietly legislating a union between Upper and Lower Canada, without so much as warning us! They would have simply brought the 420,000 Lower Canadians and the 125,000 Upper Canadians together into one "United Canada," giving equal representation to each of these two distinct identities. It was the same hare-brained scheme England had just used with ever-unruly Ireland.

From that moment on, the Patriotes realized the serious nature of this assimilationist threat of unification, against which, to be realistic, they had no legal recourse. But there were always illegal means — especially since the new French Revolution of 1830 had been snowballing not just across Europe but also here. Now the Canadiens, far from being ignorant about what was happening beyond the provincial borders, as the "philistine" school of thought would have us believe, were completely on top of all events of any significance. They proved this during the American invasion between 1775 and 1783, again during the Napoleonic victories, and yet again with the "Three Glorious Days" of 1830,[3] when our own Napoleon — born with the more prosaic name of Aimé-Nicholas Aubin — could intone that "from the St. Lawrence to the banks of the Seine, [nothing can] muffle the cry of *Liberty*."

What followed was a series of demands by the Patriotes, which were inevitably turned down by London. This led to escalating protest meetings and demonstrations, culminating finally in the 1837-38 rebellions. But that's not my field.

Gilles Gougeon: To finish up, Mr. Lahaise, you have studied the French regime in depth, as well as the transition to English rule. How would you characterize the way that nationalism quietly took root during this period?

Robert Lahaise: From the seventeenth century on, as I was saying earlier, the colonists of New France quickly adapted to the immensity of North America, as well as to the ways of the Native peoples and the cold climate. Moreover, they were no longer French, they were Canadiens, with their own accent and even their own folklore, adding to the old French tales new stories of a wintery world of forests peopled by a primitive race who were as proud as they were imperturbable. A few thousand *coureurs de bois*, missionaries and militiamen, "with hurricane-force winds for halos" as the epic writer Alfred Desrochers wrote, had been crossing North America for more than a century, and, thanks to their alliances with twenty or so First Nations, had managed until 1758 to stave off defeat against a population twenty times as large as theirs.

After 1760, we were prematurely severed from the old country, and we inevitably became closed in on ourselves. New France, contrary to the views of certain self-styled historians, was ruined. From 15,000 Acadians in 1745, there were now barely a thousand. Wolfe's troops had burned down pretty well every dwelling from the Gaspé to Quebec. In Quebec itself, only the "four houses," as people never weary of repeating, were spared by the bombardments of 1759. The massacre continued into 1760 and about a sixth of the population died either by the cannonball or from cold, hunger and epidemics, while the rest were reduced to shivering in their rags.

Understandably, the Canadian identity was radically split from that moment onwards. On the one hand, 95 per cent of the inhabitants were Francophone, Catholic, poor farmers, nostalgic for a past that they idealized, and on the other hand, there was a tiny minority of Anglophones, wealthy Protestant tradespeople with all the usual arrogance of conquerors. Add to this the weight of history that nothing could wipe out: the English and the French had been tearing each other apart ever since 1066 when William the Conqueror from Normandy seized England, and they had been doing the same in North America since 1613, the year the Virginians destroyed the Acadian settlement of Port Royal. Since then, the two solitudes have wasted time, money and energy in accusing each other of every kind of wrongdoing — it's always the minority who appear to be fanatics —

instead of designing a healthy economic collaboration crowned by a political relationship based on mutual respect.

Bibliography

Brunet, Michel. *Les Canadiens après la Conquête, 1759-1775.* Montreal: Fides, 1969.

Frégault, Guy. *La guerre de la Conquête.* Montreal: Fides, 1955.

Hamelin, Jean. *Économie et société en Nouvelle-France.* Quebec City: Presses de l'Université Laval, 1960.

Lahaise, Robert. *Histoire de la Nouvelle-France, 1524-1760.* Montreal: HMH, 1967. (In collaboration with Noël Vallerand.)

————. *Histoire de l'Amérique du Nord britannique, 1760-1867.* Montreal: HMH, 1971. (In collaboration with Noël Vallerand.)

————. *Civilisation et vie quotidienne en Nouvelle-France.* Montreal: Guérin, 1973. 1,000 slides with a book of commentary and a thematic bibliography.

Ouellet, Fernand, *Economic and Social History of Quebec 1760-1850.* Toronto: Macmillan, 1980.

Trudel, Marcel. *Initiation à la Nouvelle-France.* Montreal: Holt Rinehart and Winston, 1968.

Notes

1. François Bigot was intendant of New France from 1748 to 1760. His corruption became the stuff of legend. *–tr.*
2. Daughters of the king. *–tr.*
3. July 27-29, 1830, when the working peopl‿ ‿f Paris took control of the city, forcing the abdication of the authoritarian King Charles X and leading to the installation of Louis-Philippe, Duc d'Orléans, as constitutional monarch. *–tr.*

Interview with
Jean-Paul Bernard

Gilles Gougeon: Mr. Bernard, let us deal first with the period around 1820. Was there any nationalism to speak of during this period?

Jean-Paul Bernard: Yes, definitely. If you identify nationalism with national consciousness, or the sense of belonging to a national group, you could say it has been widespread all over the modern world. In Lower Canada this sense existed before the 1820s, and it existed afterwards, but it was in the 1820s that it began to intensify. From that time on, there was not only national consciousness but also a movement — both an ideology and its corresponding movement.

Gilles Gougeon: How did this nationalism express itself?

Jean-Paul Bernard: By and large, nationalisms assert themselves against other nationalisms rather than against their real opponent, which is cosmopolitanism. Here, within the British Empire, there were the Francophones on the one hand, who traced their origins back to French rule and were therefore an old group, and on the other hand, a newer group that was growing by leaps and bounds. These were British immigrants, whose numbers began to increase rapidly in the 1820s, with immigration reaching a peak in the 1830s. Relative to the population, this was the largest wave of immigration ever in what is now Quebec. So we're looking at a confrontation between two nationalisms, Canadien and British. In some ways neither group was really a nation, but each had hopes of becoming one. Until 1837, each side thought it had good reason to believe that it would be the central reference point around which the future of the territory would be defined.

Gilles Gougeon: There was a party around then that called itself the Parti Canadien, which at one point changed its name to the Parti Patriote. What was the significance of that?

Jean-Paul Bernard: Very simply, the term *Parti Canadien* referred first of all to the majority in the Legislative Assembly. The term came into use in the first decade of the nineteenth century. Starting in 1826, while it didn't disappear completely, it became secondary to the other name. The new name was so deeply ingrained by 1832 that the term *Parti Canadien* had disappeared.

Gilles Gougeon: Does the fact that they called themselves the Parti Patriote mean that they were more open than before, or less so?

Jean-Paul Bernard: More open. The term *Canadien* did have its exclusive aspects. At first glance, at least, it seemed you couldn't be a member of the party unless you were Canadien. At that time, the other inhabitants of Lower Canada were called "colonials" or "British Americans" (as opposed to other Americans), but they didn't call themselves Canadians. They called themselves British. The expression "French Canadian" didn't exist yet: there were the Canadiens, and then there were the British. In a sense, the primary allegiance of the British was not to this territory. They tended to define it as simply part of the British Empire. So in the commercial realm, and especially in the political realm, there were conflicts over influence and aspirations between the nationalism of the Parti Patriote, who drew inspiration from the idea of a Canadien territory and a Canadien nation, and that of a group who defined the territory as a colony of settlement for British people.

Gilles Gougeon: So it was in this context that the Patriotes emerged. What kind of country did they want?

Jean-Paul Bernard: The Parti Patriote was more like the Parti Québécois than like the Union Nationale. And I'm not just saying that to spread political propaganda!

The people who considered themselves part of the Canadien nation designated themselves as "compatriots," referring to the others as "fellow citizens" and "fellow subjects" of the British Crown. Compatriots were people of Canadien origin (except for those who didn't agree with the Patriotes' approach), along with people of other backgrounds who were more or less in agreement with their approach. And the Patriotes' approach, in the context of the British Empire, was to build what we would call now — and what they called then — a distinct society in Lower Canada. This project was not for "pure-laine"[1] French Canadians alone. It also meant coexistence with people who didn't necessarily have to speak French but who respected Canadien culture and the rights of the Canadien majority in Lower Canada. It was thus a kind of nationalism that integrated the newer elements of the population into the Canadien nation.

Gilles Gougeon: It was open —

Jean-Paul Bernard: Yes. And it was open in another way, too. Far more than later on, this nationalism was inspired by the progressive movements — what were called liberal movements at the time — of Europe and the United States.

Gilles Gougeon: So these people were democrats. They wanted a responsible government that would be tolerant in matters of language and religion. They even wanted separation of church and state —

Jean-Paul Bernard: Yes.

Gilles Gougeon: Did they want equality or ascendancy?

Jean-Paul Bernard: If you try to look at questions of equality and ascendancy together, you run into paradoxes. What some may call a hope for equality is perceived by others as a threat of ascendancy. Let me explain. We were part of the British Empire. As far as the Patriotes were concerned, the British minority was benefiting from its links with the imperial government and the significant business relationship it had established with the imperial economy. It therefore enjoyed an ascendancy that threatened the development of the Canadien nation. So in the name of equality, the Patriotes promoted the idea of democracy. They promoted the idea of a Canadien nation crying out to be freed from discrimination that favoured those who knew how to pull the imperial strings. However, if you try to see the question from the British point of view, you'll see that they perceived this assertion of Canadien nationhood not as a bid for equality but rather as a threat of Canadien ascendancy over the British minority in Lower Canada.

Gilles Gougeon: And one day the British would find a way of bringing about equality, but with the ascendancy on the other side

— this would take place in the context of an imposed union. How does 1840 fit into the development of this national self-assertion?

Jean-Paul Bernard: First, there were the rebellions of 1837-38, which were a dramatic manifestation of an old problem — a problem that had long ago been built into the very structure of the country. After the rebellions, the British came up with what was from their point of view the radical solution of uniting Upper and Lower Canada. In 1840, the British Parliament passed the Act of Union, uniting Upper and Lower Canada under one government. It would be like merging the governments, laws and institutions of present-day Quebec and Ontario into one. So they decided to unite these two political entities with the explicit, clear and publicly stated intention of putting an end to the illusion of a "Canadien nation."

The French Canadians should be compelled "to consider themselves, not as a separate body, but an integral part of a larger body," wrote John Stuart Mill, the brilliant British liberal philosopher and economist, and to "merge their nationality of race in a nationality of country; instead of French Canadians...make them British Americans." Before Mill (and the famous report to the imperial government signed by Lord Durham only confirms this), these views were held by the most militant enemies of the Parti Canadien and later the Parti Patriote. But in the name of liberalism and the smooth running of the state, Durham went beyond this proposal of reducing the French Canadians to a minority. Since the national minority's chances of survival were not that good anyway, he argued, it would be better for the individuals themselves, and for the progress and equality of all individuals in the state, if the old nationality ceded its place to the new. In other words, union and assimilation.

In fact, this assimilation never happened. But the imposed union took place, and it had its effects. It provided the institutional basis of ascendancy for the group of British origin by removing the threat in Lower Canada represented by French Canadians asserting their nationhood. Of course everyone continued to eat three meals a day even after the Union, but something had changed in terms of national status within the state. With the modification of the territory over which power was exercised, French Canadians could no longer talk in the same breath about defending democracy and nationhood or about majority rights. In that sense, ascendancy in Lower Canada did indeed change sides, and the Union, whose intention was to liberate people of British origin from possibly coming under the "tyranny of the majority," in fact consigned the French Canadians to the position of being subject to this kind of tyranny themselves.

Gilles Gougeon: In other words, from 1840 on we can see the roots of what was to become, a hundred years or so later, a very narrow form of nationalism — in the 1930s it was called undemocratic, fascist or closed in on itself.

Jean-Paul Bernard: Yes, although its development over the next hundred years was very complex and not all the factors that influenced it during that period were there in 1840. However, it's very significant that the expression *origine canadienne* started to disappear in favour of *origine canadienne-française*. This reveals a change of perspective, a forced retreat to a defensive position. This position was more conducive to defending the national characteristics of the past and also to increasing conservatism among the elites. Clericalism, for example, we know now beyond a shadow of a doubt, was something that emerged only after 1840, not before.

Gilles Gougeon: How do you account for the fact that the clergy became so important after 1840?

Jean-Paul Bernard: In the short term, it was related to the fact that the leaders involved in the rebellions, whom the clergy had disapproved of and whose downfall they had predicted, had now fallen from favour. In addition, the Catholic Church was reorganizing itself internationally to mobilize against the ideas of the French Revolution. But in the long term, and more fundamentally, it was after the Union of 1840 had left no further doubt as to the minority status of French Canadians that the church had more influence in defining the French Canadian national identity.

Gilles Gougeon: Could you summarize the aims of the Patriotes?

Jean-Paul Bernard: They wanted to get rid of abuses, notably in the granting of jobs and public lands by the colonial administration. They also wanted diversified economic development, less dependent on large imperial commercial interests. They wanted to achieve this through an elected Parliament that had primacy over the executive and legislative councils named by the British governor. Their conception of how a more or less egalitarian society should be organized is difficult to describe briefly. There was a debate within the party about seigneurial tenure,[2] for example. Their adversaries accused them of wanting to keep it, but in fact they wanted to abolish it quickly but under conditions that were extremely advantageous for the seigneurs themselves.

Gilles Gougeon: So there wasn't necessarily unanimity.

Jean-Paul Bernard: There was no unanimity. I think there is rarely unanimity over this kind of problem. Even within a united political movement, it's not as if people are all buddies and have exactly the same views.

Gilles Gougeon: What were the main things that did unite them?

Jean-Paul Bernard: I think it was the idea that to build a future in a place, you have to start with the people who are already there, while the other side tended to see it more as in a sense of a country that had yet to be created.

Gilles Gougeon: So after the Act of Union in 1840, the clergy played a more prominent role. Did they have nationalist ideas? Did they affirm the French Canadian identity in a specific way?

Jean-Paul Bernard: Yes. Of course, the clergy tended to understand the world and social organization in terms of religion, faith and their own influence. For them the primary values that should be protected and developed were religion and, along with it, language and French legal traditions. Because if people were going to move into the other group, or the other culture, or — to use the word loosely — the other society, they risked losing or letting go of their religious identity along with other elements of their identity. In statistical terms, from the French Canadian point of view in 1850, the phrase *la langue, gardienne de la foi* — language, guardian of the faith — may have described reality. There's no essential, logical relationship per se, but there is perhaps what could be called a sociological relationship, and the clergy knew it. It wasn't a ridiculous way of looking at things, but it certainly meant that nationalism would take on a *slightly* — I'm being sarcastic — clerical and conservative hue, which it didn't have before 1840.

Meanwhile a new cooperative relationship was being established among Francophone professionals, the predominantly but not exclusively Anglophone business class and the clergy, with the politicians acting as intermediaries. There was a fairly rigid upper layer that served to keep Quebec society in order after 1850-60.

Gilles Gougeon: Now that there was a union, the parliamentarians, the politicians of Lower Canada, sat in a Parliament representing the two Canadas. One of these politicians was Louis-Hippolyte Lafontaine. Did Lafontaine speak on behalf of, did he represent the Canadien or French Canadian identity in the context of this government? Was he a figure of national self-assertion or a figure of compromise?

Jean-Paul Bernard: The two were not mutually exclusive. I think he was a man who could both affirm French Canadian nationhood and make compromises. In comparing him with Papineau, Lafontaine's dominant tendencies may have been different. Perhaps Papineau's assertion of nationhood was more unswerving, and Lafontaine's ability to compromise was relatively greater. In the historical literature — more among past historians than contemporary ones — there has been great emphasis on Lafontaine's glorious deed, which was to declare before the gathering of Parliament in Kingston after Union that, although French wasn't an official language under Union law, he was going to speak it anyway. "I owe it to my compatriots," he said, "and I owe it to myself." Okay, so he was being somewhat bold. But using Papineau as our point of comparison, Lafontaine is the one who had to give in. In his first election speech after Union he said "Canada is the land of our ancestors; it is our homeland, as it must be the adopted homeland of the various people who come...to settle here."

Gilles Gougeon: Whatever their origins —

Jean-Paul Bernard: "Their children will have to be, like us, Canadian first and foremost," Lafontaine went on. This declaration was linked to his belief that on an economic level, this would encourage "the development of our vast resources." And it's understandable that in terms of raising capital on the English market, things would be easier this way. And, in fact, the Act of Union was also a financial transaction, closely watched over by the giant British financial house of Baring and Glyn, to which Upper Canada was deeply in debt.

Gilles Gougeon: And Lower Canada wasn't.

Jean-Paul Bernard: Lower Canada spent less on public works. It came into the Union with fewer assets but also a much smaller debt.

Gilles Gougeon: Between 1840 and 1867, was there a feeling among French Canadians that "if you can't beat them, join them," as the Americans say? Let's try to play the game, let's try and fit into this new country — or were there hesitations?

Jean-Paul Bernard: Actually, there were elements of federalism from 1841-42 on, when the institutions of the Province of Canada were being established. In general, after having initially despaired of the future, they now said "Oh, it'll be all right." They decided that things were not as tragic as they had seemed. The idea caught on that they would be able to get by with what they had, and that they could survive in a way that wouldn't be so painful. Then there were the *Rouges* who, starting in 1847-48, tried to resurrect the radical nationalism of the past and struggle against the emergence of clericalism. But the situation had changed, and they had a lot of difficulty coming up with an alternative program.

The Rouges ended up thinking, only for a short while of course, that the only solution to the problems of French Canada was to be annexed to the United States. Their adversaries thought this was an illogical idea, but it was more the logic of despair. In other words, if we're going to disappear as a collectivity, a community, a society, we might as well disappear completely into a larger and richer universe that would give us more individual opportunity, more chance to fulfil our personal ambitions. The Rouges declared at that point that ties with the United States would be better than the forced link with English Canada as it stood in the 1840s. With Confederation, the whole of British North America became the Dominion of Canada, which they came close (I'm exaggerating) to naming Northalia, in contrast to Australia. The original Canada, the Canada of the *nation canadienne*, had given way to another Canada.

Gilles Gougeon: So they were going to change the name.

Jean-Paul Bernard: And changing the name would have been a clear sign, something that would have attracted people's attention and made them realize that they hadn't understood a lot of what was going on.

Gilles Gougeon: Whom do you mean when you speak of the Rouges? Who were their leaders? Who were the important figures in the movement?

Jean-Paul Bernard: Looking at the Rouges as a political party, their most important leader was Antoine-Aimé Dorion, who wasn't a very striking character. But they were also a cultural group, who together with the Institut Canadien formed a cooperative cultural association, with its own lectures, books, a library in Montreal that lent books, et cetera.

Gilles Gougeon: They were the freethinkers of their time.

Jean-Paul Bernard: Yes. The most brilliant figure among the Rouges of the Institut Canadien was Louis-Antoine Dessaulles, Papineau's nephew. And in the late 1860s Papineau himself kept in touch with the Institut Canadien in Montreal. It was a refuge for him during those years — elsewhere, he was a nobody. No one was thinking the way he thought any more. In fact, the general feeling was that anticlerical liberal democrats like Papineau were a bit of a pain. French Canadian nationalism had moved on. From 1842 onward, Joseph-Édouard Cauchon, MP for Montmorency and editor of the *Journal de Québec*, contrasted Papineau's skill in rooting out abuses in the past with the duty henceforth to act constructively for the needs of the future.

Bibliography

Bernard, Jean-Paul. *Les Rouges: Libéralisme, nationalisme et anti-cléricalisme au milieu du XIXme siècle*. Montreal: Presses de l'Université du Québec, 1971.
————. *Les Rebellions de 1837-1838: Les Patriotes dans la mémoire collective et chez les historiens*. Montreal: Boréal Express, 1983.

Durham, John George Lambton, Earl of. *Lord Durham's Report: An Abridgement of Report on the Affairs of British North America.* Edited and with an introduction by Gerald M. Craig. Toronto: McClelland and Stewart, 1963.

Journal of Canadian Studies/Revue d'Études canadiennes 25, no. 1 (Spring 1990). Special issue on Durham — the man and his ideas.

Monet, Jacques. *La première révolution tranquille: Le nationalisme canadien-français (1837-1850).* Montreal: Fides, 1981.

Ouellet, Fernand. *Le Bas-Canada 1791-1840: Changements structuraux et crises.* Ottawa: Éditions de l'Université d'Ottawa, 1976.

Notes

1. Literally "pure wool." The term is used for old-stock French Canadians as opposed to any of the ethnic groups that have come to Quebec since the British takeover. *–tr.*

2. The semi-feudal system of land tenure established under the French regime, retained by the British and finally abolished on terms favourable to the seigneurs in 1854. *–tr.*

Part Two

The second program shows how, between 1867 and 1917, the "Canadiens" (or Francophones) believed in a Canada that had been conceived in 1867, a vision which conflicted with that of the "English" (native-born or immigrant Anglophones), who saw their country as a branch of the British Empire. The Louis Riel affair, the Boer War, and conscription in 1917 are the key events, and it was through these events that Wilfrid Laurier, Henri Bourassa, Honoré Mercier and the early "indépendantistes" became prominent.

The interview is with historian Réal Bélanger.

Interview with Réal Bélanger

Gilles Gougeon: Mr. Bélanger, first of all I'd like you to put us in the context of 1867. A new political, economic and social dynamic had just been created — so what was the meaning of 1867?

Réal Bélanger: From the perspective of French Canadians, 1867 represented a number of different realities. Of course it signified the establishment of the federal structure and the means by which the newly created nation — that is the Canadian nation — could thrive. This nation, as far as French Canadians were concerned, was to be bilingual and bicultural and was to accept the equality of the two founding peoples of Canada. In this spirit, as they saw it, 1867 also represented an agreement. It was a pact between the provinces and the federal government, but it was also a pact between these two founding peoples of Canada, who would respect each other in the future, and who together, everywhere in this great land in the making, would be able to achieve great economic ventures and other great things.

At the same time, many French Canadians realized in 1867 that politically, as only one province among four, Quebec was a minority in the new federal structure, and they believed their situation could only get worse. An equally important observation went along with this: Confederation also meant that French Canadians had finally obtained a provincial state. The province of Quebec was a state, a stable environment in which French Canadians could concentrate on preserving the characteristics that defined them: their language, their Catholic faith, their culture, their institutions, their laws and their way of life. Quebec's autonomy was regarded as being of the highest importance because it represented an end to the pernicious Act of Union of 1840-41. Let me stress that at the time, French Canadians were quite certain that they could form a distinct nation within this new Canada, a nation that would be based on the characteristics I just mentioned.

Gilles Gougeon: Are there texts that corroborate that?

Réal Bélanger: I can show you plenty of texts that say so. I would also add that in 1867, and even more so in the years that followed, French Canadians understood very well that the province of Quebec would be at the heart of this distinct nation. It was against this backdrop that the development of French Canadian nationalisms between 1867 and 1920 played themselves out. A number of events produced this backdrop, not the least of which was repeated episodes of provocation by the English Canadian majority.

You'll notice that I refer to several nationalisms, not just one. As you'll see in the course of this conversation, there were in fact many kinds of French Canadian nationalism. They represent a rupture with the preceding era in some ways, but there are continuities as well.

Gilles Gougeon: If you don't mind, let's talk about Tardivel, a man I'd like you to describe in the context of his own era. Who was Tardivel?

Réal Bélanger: Jules-Paul Tardivel was born in the United States and moved to Quebec in 1868, at the age of seventeen, to pursue classical studies at the Saint-Hyacinthe seminary and to learn French. He expressed much of his thought through his newspaper *La Vérité*, which he published from 1881 until his death in 1905. But to grasp the significance of his thinking, you need to place him in the context of the thinking of his day, particularly the dominant cultural and conservative nationalism.

His basic principle was the preservation of the Catholic religion, the French language and institutions, and French Canadian law and history. His thinking was also based on the defence of a conservative society resistant to the idea of liberalism. It was centred on a rural and agricultural way of life, which could come to terms with a certain degree of industrialization, but only if it was connected to agriculture or to natural resources. The idea of *survivance* emerges clearly, but there was more to it than that. There was also the evangelical mission of the French Canadian nation on the North American continent, and — something often overlooked by researchers — the idea of peacefully reconquering the territory lost in 1760.

Tardivel subscribed to this brand of nationalism. But in some respects he pushed it to extremes. As an ultramontane, he placed the Catholic faith right at the centre of the defining characteristics of the French Canadian nation. In fact, for him, the Catholic religion embraced all the other characteristics, which in Tardivel's view were subordinate to it. He concluded that the spiritual should take precedence over the temporal, and that the church should dominate the state. In fact, Tardivel's ultramontane nationalism went even further than that. He added political extremism to his religious and social extremism, and that was what really isolated him in his own time.

Gilles Gougeon: At the time, was nationalism as politicized as it became subsequently?

Réal Bélanger: Although we should be careful not to generalize about how politicized different forms of nationalism were in this era, I totally disagree with people who maintain that nineteenth-century nationalisms were apolitical. These researchers make this claim rather too blithely, without having sufficiently explored the newspapers and archives of the day. If they examined these documents really carefully they would modify their claims substantially.

They would certainly discover that for Tardivel himself, the political component of his nationalism was one of its fundamental elements, and this was his single most original contribution. In fact, Tardivel went on to draw up the first separatist program in the history of Canadian Confederation. It was a coherent, duly constituted program, but it differed from the one the Patriotes, whom you have discussed with other historians, put forward before 1867. So Tardivel's nationalism was not truncated. It formed a cultural and political entity cemented together by the religious dimension.

Gilles Gougeon: But why did Tardivel believe that the only solution was separatism?

Réal Bélanger: Until 1885, Tardivel accepted Confederation because he saw in it a political structure that gave Quebec the autonomy it needed to develop as a French Canadian, Catholic society. He supported the idea of a provincial state subordinate to the federal state and the imperial state. Then between 1885 and 1890 he came to reject Confederation completely. Why? Beyond considering his combative personality, we also need to look at a line of argument based on several mutually reinforcing elements. First, he was very fearful that Quebec was becoming more and more of a minority in Canada. In 1885, it was already reduced to one province among seven in the country, and where its population had been 32.3 per cent of Canada's total in 1871, it was down to 30.8 per cent in 1890.

Tardivel was also increasingly aware that the English Canadians were not inclined to respect the *bonne entente* concluded in 1867. And it was French Canadians outside Quebec who bore the brunt of this, as their religious, linguistic and educational rights were being ignored. In 1871 the problem manifested itself in New Brunswick, and then between 1885 and 1890 it spread westward to Manitoba and as far as the Northwest Territories. Tardivel feared the worst for French Canadians outside Quebec, but he also suspected that one day Quebec itself would be confronted with the threat of the Anglophone Protestant Orangemen and Freemasons. His worry increased with his growing awareness of the centralist tendencies of the federal government under John A. Macdonald, whom Tardivel abhorred because "that Freemason," as he called him, was undermining the very foundations of provincial autonomy.

He was also of the opinion that Quebec ought to remain rural and agricultural, but it was in the process of becoming a little too industrial and urban. On top of that, Canada was unable to provide enough help in stopping the massive tide of French Canadian emigration to the United States.

This helps us understand better what led the publisher of *La Vérité* to come to the conclusion that Confederation was, as he later wrote, a geographic absurdity of the first order. But what triggered this conclusion, catalysing his vigorous opposition to Confederation and leading him to take a separatist position, was the hanging of the Métis Louis Riel on November 16, 1885. This became the major drama of the decade, and it was at this point that Tardivel first put forward his plan for separation.

How shall I describe this plan to you? First of all, beyond the cultural and social elements of Tardivel's nationalism that I mentioned earlier and that he still subscribed to, he wanted to make Quebec a separate state, capable of putting the full measure of ultramontane fundamentalism into practice. It would be a true Catholic nation-state, independent of Canada (but not of England, which could still protect us), and it would resist annexation by the United States. But it would maintain economic ties with Canada, such as a customs union, for example. It would have the advantage of a larger territory, not just the existing Province of Quebec, but also the French areas of the northeastern United States and eastern Canada. Tardivel saw it, in a sense, as representing the renaissance of the former New France — the hope for reconquest.

However, he shed precious little light on how this separate state would function, except we know that he rejected the Canadian parliamentary system and leaned towards presidential government, with dictatorial overtones but subject to the authority of the church. We know, too, that he favoured respecting the minorities who were already established here but rejected any amalgamation with them, and, in the long term, the state that he envisaged was homogeneously French Canadian. This ideal state would come into being peacefully, with no threat to anyone and at God's appointed time — around 1950, he figured. Tardivel passionately urged French Canadians to prepare for this great day, and he suggested a vigorous course of action in the meantime.

Gilles Gougeon: Did Tardivel's thought hold much sway? Was he listened to and understood by the people?

Réal Bélanger: I'd say that in some aspects of his nationalism, especially its cultural and conservative basis, Tardivel was in tune with many of his contemporaries. As a result, although he took an extremist position on these topics, too, these elements of his thought exercised a certain influence on the French Canadian people and contributed to their developing a sense of collective identity. In this respect I think he prepared the way for future leaders such as Henri Bourassa and Lionel Groulx, and also for future movements of which the most persistent was the Association de la Jeunesse Catholique Canadienne-Française (French Canadian Catholic Youth Association).

The picture changes, of course, when you look at the political aspect of his nationalism and his proposal for the separation of Quebec. Here, how you judge his influence depends on the time frame you look at. In his own time, Tardivel had very little influence and remained a marginal figure in society. He had no following among the political figures of his day. In 1903 his newspaper *La Vérité* had 3,000 subscribers, but they were mostly priests and professors. Only 5 per cent of them were working-class. The large majority of French Canadians preferred the political system in place. But in the medium and long term, this aspect of his nationalism had a slightly greater impact in some ways — first in 1922, when Abbé Lionel Groulx's Action Française group flirted with the idea of independence, and then in the thirties, when groups like Jeunes-Canada (Canada Youth), the newspaper *La Nation* and individuals such as Dostaler O'Leary were unabashedly discussing independence. Today the idea of separatism is bandied about all the time, but its sociocultural roots are quite different from the kind of separatism that Tardivel was talking about.

Despite these qualifications, I think it's safe to say that Jules-Paul Tardivel was the father of separatist thought under Confederation, and along with Honoré Mercier he remains the dominant figure in French Canadian nationalism during the decades immediately following Confederation.

Gilles Gougeon: You mentioned Louis Riel. Louis Riel lived far away from Quebec — how do you account for the repercussions that the Métis rebellion had here and for the effects of his hanging? How does Louis Riel fit into the history of nationalism?

Réal Bélanger: I believe Riel was very important, as he was both a flash point and a catalyst. If Riel was so significant, it's because French Canadians of the time and their political leaders thought — rightly or not, but they did — that this person and the event in which he was caught up were part of the continuing struggle between French Canadians, who of course were trying to retain their rights and nationality within this country, and English Canadians.

 When Riel was hanged on November 16, 1885, it was definitely seen as a direct hit on a fellow French Canadian. And people like Tardivel and Honoré Mercier loudly proclaimed it as such. The two of them said that Riel, our brother, was executed because he was French Canadian and a Catholic. So you can imagine what kind of position this gave Riel in the history of French Canadian nationalism.

It was from this moment that Tardivel became openly separatist, and it was then, too, that Honoré Mercier set in motion a real nationalist movement and his celebrated Parti National. The party was made up of Liberals and Conservatives who agreed to unite to better defend the French Canadian nation and help fulfil its aspirations. The same momentum propelled Mercier into office as premier of Quebec in January 1887.

So the Riel affair was a crucial event, but it has another significance, too. From that point onward, French Canadians increasingly understood that the federal government wasn't always — and maybe less and less — going to protect them under Confederation. They had already taken note of its inaction over the New Brunswick schools question, which they were about to see repeated in Manitoba. They grasped that the federal government was not, after all, the great protector of their rights. It was the start of a kind of withdrawal back to Quebec, but above all it produced a strengthened conviction that Quebec was really the heart of the French Canadian nation — the place where, for the time being, they were most protected. And clearly, Quebec was the place where their rights must not be compromised because, in time, the existence of the homeland itself could be endangered.

Gilles Gougeon: You refer to the Manitoba and New Brunswick schools questions. Could you sum up the debate around separate schools and its importance, both real and symbolic, for French Canadians?

Réal Bélanger: When historians refer to the schools debate in New Brunswick and Manitoba, they're talking about a debate over the rights of the Catholic minority to separate schools in those provinces — that is, the right to publicly funded denominational schools catering to a province's religious minorities. Now the Catholic minorities in those two provinces, who were Irish and French Canadian, effectively lost their right to separate schools between 1871 and 1890. Note that the debate wasn't primarily about the French language — that argument would break out a little later, with Regulation 17 in Ontario around 1912. Rather, this debate was concerned with the Catholic religion, one of the fundamental characteristics of the French Canadian nation. To attack Catholicism was an affront to the French Canadian nationality itself.

Gilles Gougeon: Then what happened? French Canadians wanted Catholic schools and others didn't. Didn't the provinces want them?

Réal Bélanger: That's what the situation was. Until then French Canadian Catholics, and Irish Catholics too, had had the benefit of separate schools in the two provinces concerned. But under pressure from the Protestant English Canadian majority, which rejected the spirit of the 1867 Constitution, the government of New Brunswick in 1871 and the government of Manitoba in 1890 established a system of public nondenominational schools, which effectively led to the abolition of separate Catholic schools. Running counter even to its own provincial constitution, the government of Manitoba in 1890 went so far as to abolish French as an official language.

That wasn't what caused the protests of the Catholic minority, however. Their demands, as I say, were over the problem of separate schools. And then there were protests. In the case of separate schools in Manitoba, they lasted from 1890 to 1897, and French Canadians in Quebec unhesitatingly supported the cause of their brothers in the west. As it turned out, the protests came to nothing in New Brunswick, and to very little in Manitoba.

In view of this fairly disappointing outcome, French Canadians in Quebec, or at least most of them, were no longer under any illusions about the intentions of the English Canadian majority. In 1897 they knew for sure that their misgivings about the future sparked by the Riel affair were now more pertinent than ever, and that they must not be forgotten. They also knew that English Canadians were all set to do battle for a unicultural, English-speaking Canada. That issue was coming, and they knew it.

Gilles Gougeon: What was Bill 17 in Ontario?

Réal Bélanger: That was a little later, in 1912. Actually it was a regulation, Regulation 17, which Ontario adopted and which was a devastating blow to the French Canadian minority in the province. In Ontario, the English Canadians left the issue of denominational schools alone and instead attacked the French schools, or bilingual schools as they called them. A direct offspring of the truncated version of the country that the English Canadian majority was trying to impose, the Regulation had the effect of limiting the use of French as a language of instruction and communication to the first two years of elementary school. In practice, it led to the almost complete abolition of instruction in French in the Ontario bilingual schools.

Imagine the outcry this provoked among the French Canadian minority in Ontario! Imagine the outcry in Quebec! The resistance of the Franco-Ontarians was quite remarkable, all in all, and they were supported by the French Canadians in Quebec, both by the political elite — people such as Henri Bourassa, Armand Lavergne, Lomer Gouin and Wilfrid Laurier — and by other kinds of people in Quebec society. Quebec's support was very active, starting in 1912 and lasting through the whole of the First World War: political meetings proliferated; funds were raised; there were lively discussions about the "casualties in Ontario" and attacks on the so-called "Ontario Huns." But it was all to no avail. In Quebec and in Francophone Ontario more than a few French Canadians figured that

Regulation 17 just confirmed their suspicions of the English Canadians' evil intentions regarding the future definition of Canada.

Gilles Gougeon: So in this context, there were political figures in Quebec who co-opted these protest movements. I'm thinking of Honoré Mercier — who was Honoré Mercier?

Réal Bélanger: I should first point out that the most important moments in Mercier's career took place a little before the events I've been describing, more in the years 1880 to 1894. Who was Honoré Mercier? At first he was a political Conservative who opposed Canadian Confederation in 1867; then he became a Liberal activist and then leader of the Liberal Party in 1883. At that time it was a weak party. It was ravaged by divisions, and the Catholic clergy still feared its radicalism, mild as that radicalism was.

To really understand Honoré Mercier's nationalism, you have to see how strongly the sociopolitical atmosphere of Quebec affected him — I mean the same elements that shaped the development of Tardivel's nationalist thought and led him to seriously question the future of Confederation in the 1880s. I don't want to repeat myself, but to understand Mercier's actions from these years forward it's important to keep at least some aspects of this political reality in mind. Above all, it was the hanging of Louis Riel on November 16, 1885, that provoked the strongest reaction in Mercier, as it did in Tardivel. Mercier then took the helm of the nationalist movement in Quebec that was launched in protest against the hanging, against its causes and possible after-effects. He even formed a new political party, made up of Liberals and dissident Conservatives who disagreed with the official party position that had led to the hanging. Mercier reached the pinnacle of his career on January 29, 1887, when he became premier of Quebec. He stayed in the post until 1891, when the government was thrown out of office over the Baie des Chaleurs scandal.[1]

Gilles Gougeon: What was his influence or his role in Quebec's national self-assertion?

Réal Bélanger: Mercier was a flamboyant politician with great panache, and you could say he was the father of the idea of Quebec autonomy. It is thanks to him that this idea became the political expression of French Canadian nationalism. But let's start at the beginning. How did Mercier's particular brand of nationalism manifest itself? First of all, after the fashion of nationalisms of his era, through vigorous defence of the cultural characteristics of the French Canadian nation that I spoke of earlier. Mercier, you see, was proud of his nation and of French Canadians, and he didn't hold back from making passionate speeches on the subject. He would shout from the hustings phrases like "This province is Catholic and French and will remain Catholic and French!" And Mercier suggested a way to be sure it would come to pass: "My French Canadian brothers, let us cease our fratricidal strife and unite!" In addition, Mercier put many of his liberal ideals on hold, partly out of conviction and partly out of political opportunism. This allowed him to fit in better with the prevailing social conservatism and be more in tune with the ultramontanes and with society in general. However, he also pursued economic development for Quebec, and modernized it slightly in some ways. He increased government investment and tried to modernize agriculture to bring it into the market economy. He took action on colonization and education. All in all, Mercier put into effect a fully developed, wide-ranging cultural nationalism.

And he didn't stop there, of course. He added a political dimension to this cultural nationalism, and this dimension was very important to him. The inspiration for this dimension was the political development of Confederation, which I spoke of earlier, and the development of the federal-provincial relationship. Mercier was inspired by the idea that the rights of French Canadians could only truly be protected in Quebec, and inspired too by Justice Loranger's famous *Lettres sur l'interprétation de la Constitution*, in which he maintained that since it was the provinces that had created the federal government in the first place, it should be subordinate to them. All this inspired Mercier to stand up for the Quebec state and to demand that Ottawa respect its autonomy — this demand was a first in the political life of Quebec. In fact, until 1887, it was Ontario that had shown the strongest tendency towards autonomy in federal-provincial relations. But from 1887 onwards, Mercier distinguished himself in this field. That year he convened the first interprovincial conference in the history of Confederation. From then on, autonomy became the rallying cry of French Canadian nationalism. Mercier of course defended it on every front with considerable pomp and grandeur, and at great cost, in his inimitable style. He was even bold enough to want international recognition for Quebec.

Gilles Gougeon: When Honoré Mercier talked of autonomy though, he didn't mean separation. Did he always see Quebec staying within Confederation?

Réal Bélanger: You're right. When Mercier talked about Quebec autonomy, he wasn't speaking of separation. Like other nationalist thinkers of his time, except for Tardivel, Mercier believed in Canada and in the federal structure. He believed that the French Canadian nation must express itself within Confederation, but a Confederation that would respect Quebec's autonomy. There's no doubt about it.

Gilles Gougeon: Did he always believe in Confederation?

Réal Bélanger: He always did. At certain crucial moments in his career, between 1885 and his death in 1894, the positions he took and his inflammatory speeches led many English Canadians to take him for a separatist, a politician who wanted to found an independent state of Quebec. But that wasn't Mercier's objective, even if he did occasionally voice some reservations about Confederation and the behaviour of the English Canadian majority in Canada. When Mercier discussed independence, he was thinking more in terms of the Empire. He wanted to break the ties that bound Canada to the British Empire. He wanted Canada to become an independent country.

Gilles Gougeon: During this era one figure started to stand out: Henri Bourassa. He was in the same camp as Honoré Mercier at that point. Tell us a little about Henri Bourassa and his influence.

Réal Bélanger: Henri Bourassa is an important figure who had considerable influence in Quebec. In the early twentieth century he was the most prominent nationalist leader in the province. He developed into the mentor of a nationalist movement that would both ignite the fervour of Quebec and provoke the opposition of English Canada.

It was in 1899 that he really became a figure on the Canadian political scene. He was elected to the federal Parliament in 1896 for the riding of Labelle, and he made his presence felt in the House of Commons and in Quebec in 1899 with his reaction to Laurier's position on Canadian participation in the Boer War.

This famous war in South Africa pitted the English against the Boers, who were Dutch settlers living in the Transvaal and the Orange Free State. Laurier had decided to help England by sending

Canadian volunteers to South Africa. Bourassa objected strenuously to this *fait accompli.* He challenged Laurier's actions, resigned from the House and was immediately re-elected by a large majority in Labelle. When he returned to the House, he kicked up a huge row to begin his resounding career.

Bourassa undertook all this in the name of nationalism, but of a kind that clashed with English Canadian nationalism, which was just as vigorous in its own way, and which I'll get to later. In overall terms, how should Henri Bourassa's nationalism be interpreted? It was a pan-Canadian nationalism, so it wasn't confined to Quebec territory. "*La patrie* [the homeland]," wrote Bourassa, "*c'est le Canada.*" His nationalism was a defence of the Canadian nation as it had been conceived in 1867 — that is, a bilingual and bicultural nation composed of and respected by the two founding peoples equally. Clearly, this included French Canadians everywhere in Canada, with their own particular deep-rooted characteristics.

He saw this Canadian nation as tending towards social conservatism centred on a limited form of economic development, carried out by and for Canadians themselves. But there was another very important element in Bourassa's nationalist thought. The Canadian nation, which now belonged to the British Empire, must get rid of its colonial ties. Canada must reject any imperial federation and ultimately achieve full independence by breaking with England. He saw independence as one of the few avenues towards fulfilling all the hopes of the nation whose strength was his chief goal. That was Bourassa's nationalism and the way he proposed to define the Canadian nation. But don't forget, this nation was made up of English Canadians and French Canadians equally, and Bourassa wanted French Canadians to flourish both in Quebec and in Canada as a whole. So in purely cultural terms, Bourassa was in line with some of the nationalisms I described earlier.

Gilles Gougeon: But why was fighting the Boer War at odds with the expression of Canadian nationalism?

Réal Bélanger: Because to Bourassa, it called into question Canada's place in the British Empire and its evolution towards independent statehood. And to help understand Bourassa's reaction, I should describe the kind of nationalism that was prevalent in English Canada, which is what he was up against in the first decades of the twentieth century.

Broadly speaking, this form of nationalism sought a Canada that would be British above all, unilingually English, Protestant and uni-cultural. Under this definition, French Canadians would be tolerated in Quebec but must not be allowed to impose their point of view or their nationality outside Quebec. These nationalists, who saw themselves as being on the progressive side socially and economically, wanted the Canadian nation to flourish, of course, but thought that at this stage it could only happen under the aegis of the British Empire. The more closely tied Canada was to the Empire, they reasoned, the more quickly it could gain enough strength to meet its other aim, which was to become a fully developed, sovereign nation.

So this form of nationalism, which we call imperialist, had the same ends as Henri Bourassa's, but the means were different. Canada's best chance of gaining independence, the imperialists believed, lay in sticking close to the Empire, which was strong and solid (and Canada would always have to stand up for it, by the way) and which might even develop into an imperial federation. So this was the English Canadian brand of nationalism, and it exerted a lot of pressure on Laurier to help the English in their war against the Boers. By acting in the spirit of this nationalism, Canada would be shoring up England and the Empire and — better still — making a name for itself and consolidating its own strength at the same time.

This was clearly not Bourassa's position. For him, Canada's participation in the Boer War was a step backward, away from independent statehood, as it showed Canada as a colony marching to orders from England. Moreover, this was a dangerous precedent that could draw Canada into fighting future wars on England's side. These arguments were at the heart of Bourassa's nationalism, and to get back to your question, he expressed them right from the start. He didn't refrain from warning the Canadian people against Laurier's position and the imperialist idea. But it was no use.

This is why Bourassa backed the founding of the Ligue National-iste Canadienne in 1903 by young people such as Olivar Asselin, Armand Lavergne, Jules Fournier and Omer Héroux, who started up the Ligue to advance their ideas. From those turbulent years onwards, Henri Bourassa became the leading nationalist figure in Quebec, and remained so at least until 1920.

Gilles Gougeon: Laurier, who was French Canadian, was prime minister during this time. Wasn't he torn between the deep longings that he saw among French Canadians and his own desire to be leader, to be the prime minister, of a country that was increasingly Anglophone?

Réal Bélanger: I'd say that Laurier was torn all his life on this subject. All his life he would say that he, a French Canadian, never should have been the leader of a federal party in Canada, a country that was so complex and difficult to lead. The two founding peoples' divergent positions on such fundamental questions was a major concern of Laurier's.

Take, for example, the French Canadians and their nationalist aspirations within Canada. Laurier understood these aspirations only too well, as he himself had been a bitter opponent of Canadian Confederation between 1864 and 1867. He had written some stirring lines on the subject, calling Confederation the death-knell of the French Canadian nation. Of course later on, as a result of a number of different circumstances, he came around to Confederation. But someone who had thought like that and written such words was no stranger to the nationalist sentiments of his compatriots. And when he became prime minister in 1896, on the whole they had faith in him. Laurier knew very well what he represented to French Canadians: feelings of pride, and also a sense of revenge for the defeat of 1759-60. He knew that Quebec nationalists of various stripes — except for Tardivel of course, who saw him as a traitor to his people — were very happy to see him installed as head of government. Laurier knew all this and it pleased him enormously, so he didn't want to disappoint them.

But Laurier also realized one thing above all when he became prime minister: he was prime minister of the entire country, of all Canadians and not just French Canadians, not just those whose goal was a flourishing French Canadian nation. He was also prime minister of the English Canadians and of their particular brand of nationalism. Consequently, Laurier knew that he had to rise above his own ideas and arbitrate between the different types of nationalism in the country and, especially after 1900, between the two principal tendencies that I discussed earlier. Caught between the two groups, Laurier claimed to represent the middle road. But I think this was a terribly difficult balance to hold, and he ended up tilting too often to the side of the English Canadian majority. There are striking examples of this throughout Laurier's time in office, which was from 1896 to 1911.

Gilles Gougeon: Let's take a look at some of these examples: the Manitoba schools, the Ontario situation, the Boer War. Did Laurier tend only towards a pan-Canadian political stance or did he also protect the political and social interests of French Canadians?

Réal Bélanger: I want to answer that by returning briefly to my last answer. Laurier always said — I quote from memory: "I want to position myself at the centre of all the political positions current in this country. As head of the government of Canada, I must appeal to a spirit of compromise that will enable me to react better to all the different pressures on me and will help me achieve national unity. For the main aim of my political career is to unite this Canada, this bilingual bicultural nation, which one day, at the opportune time and not before we are really ready, will secure its independence from England."

Consequently Laurier embraced a pan-Canadian nationalism, which I would say — and which he said — steered a middle course. He would always, as he said, resist the idea of a purely British Canada with imperial leanings, just as he would always resist Bourassa's ideas, which he believed were too upsetting to the traditions of the English Canadian majority.

In the long run, he concluded, it was best to stick to his chosen route of political compromise, as he did with the Manitoba schools question, the schools issue in Alberta and Saskatchewan, the Boer War, et cetera. As he took this course he also emphasized, for the benefit of French Canadians, that it was the bicultural character of the nation, it was them and their rights that he was protecting in both the short and the long term. And if one day their rights were attacked in Quebec itself, his policy of compromise would prove decisive in their defence.

Gilles Gougeon: But did he protect them, or was he, in fact, against their rights?

Réal Bélanger: I'm getting around to that — a historian's answer always has to take into account a full understanding of the era and the historical figures who were involved in these issues. In all the cases I've listed, Laurier certainly wasn't against French Canadian Catholics and he sincerely hoped he could protect them. But Laurier was also a man in power, a man of government, and the head of a political party that was dominated by English Canadians. He had to conform to that reality, just as he had to conform to the delicate situation of a country where ethnic divisions were so prominent.

In the end, I believe, Laurier was so eager to compromise at any cost, his fudging was so constant, and his political opportunism so great, that he was induced to go against even his own version of Canadian nationalism. This led to the virtual ruin of the dreams of Canadian dualism that were written into the 1867 Constitution and that Laurier believed in, and to the acceptance of the English Canadian majority's truncated version of Canada's nationhood. In the process, Laurier got English Canadians accustomed to winning all their battles on the question.

So I don't think Laurier was against French Canadians in Quebec or outside Quebec, but the long and short of it is that he didn't protect them, in spite of what he said. His compromises, which were really a series of retreats, led towards a strategy of trying to achieve our ends small step by small step. Their ultimate result, in our own time, was the federal political strategy of 1980 and 1982, whose consequences we know so well.[2]

Let's take the example of separate schools in Alberta and Saskatchewan. I haven't spoken about this episode yet, but it was crucial in the history of Canada, of the Canadian nation. When Laurier created the two western provinces of Alberta and Saskatchewan in 1905, he was prepared to give the Catholic minority of the two provinces the right to separate schools. But when he introduced a bill in Parliament to that effect, the English Canadian majority raised such a hue and cry that he had to revoke his decision, change his position in the House of Commons and accept yet another lame compromise that considerably limited the right to separate schools in the two provinces. "I saved the status quo, at least," he wrote privately. Perhaps it was true. But just imagine if instead Laurier's original bill was passed because he had the political will to stick with it to the end. Imagine what that would have done for the chances of the dualist vision of 1867 to be realized in large measure. Just imagine for a minute what that would have meant for western Canada today. But it wasn't to be, and that's why the question that arose in 1905 is so significant. Laurier came around, so to speak, to the Canadianization of the West according to English Canadians' vision and in their fashion. What happened in 1905 was the culmination of all the ordeals suffered by the minorities outside Quebec. The last chance to build a truly bicultural country had been blown.

Gilles Gougeon: Yet when he became leader of the opposition a little later, and when the conscription issue came up in 1917, Laurier changed his position. Wasn't Laurier opposed to conscription?

Réal Bélanger: Yes. As leader of the opposition in 1917, Laurier rejected the military conscription of Canadians and thus at last gave a clear signal that he was coming around to a French Canadian position. But to properly understand Laurier's reaction to conscription in 1917, you have to go back to his thoughts on the links between Canada and the Empire, and it helps to know something of what went on between 1909 and 1917.

Laurier's thoughts on the relationship between Canada and the Empire can be summed up as follows: He hoped that one day, when the time was ripe, Canada would gain its independence from the Empire. But in the meantime this country should resist imperialist onslaughts and take advantage of any opportunities to improve its status as a nation within the Empire — which at this stage, in spite of everything, we had to defend. All the while we should maintain our own national unity, which was so crucial to the kind of development we sought. It was with these ideas in mind that Laurier launched his famous navy in 1910 when England said it was being threatened by Germany.

He announced that he would try to prevent the overzealous imperialists from offering excessive help to the threatened motherland, but at the same time he didn't succumb to nationalist pressure from Henri Bourassa, who didn't believe in the German threat and insisted on keeping to the status quo. Laurier added that the navy would enable Canada to take one more step towards full nationhood, as it showed that Canada was a country that could contribute to its own defence and really had the capacity to do so. In doing all of this Canada would also, in its own way, be supporting the British Empire, and under the circumstances this level of support could be considered fair and acceptable.

Laurier took a similar approach to Canadian participation in the 1914-18 war. In 1914, the great majority of Canadians, Laurier included, supported the voluntary involvement of Canadians in the war to help England and France — the two motherlands — defeat Germany. Even Henri Bourassa was in agreement, as long as Canada was capable. People in Quebec were as enthusiastic as people in Toronto. But as you know, the war lasted well beyond 1914, and all kinds of problems arose. Economic problems, of course, but also problems having to do with recruiting enough soldiers for this inter-minable war that kept demanding more overseas reinforcements. It wasn't the war itself that was at issue, but rather the extent of Canada's involvement. In 1917 the question was: Should Canada go as far as military conscription in helping England and the Allies win the war? The majority of English Canadians, who were more impe-rialist, responded in the affirmative. The majority of French Canadi-ans, led by Henri Bourassa and his nationalists, replied in the negative. Prime Minister Borden responded to the wishes of the English Canadian majority and in the summer of 1917 presented a bill in Parliament to this end.

For once Laurier joined the majority of French Canadians, and he rejected conscription. Why was this? First of all because Laurier, who was basically a tolerant man, was not disposed to accept such an idea as conscription. It repelled him all the more in that conscrip-tion, inspired by the imperialist wave and vigorously opposed by French Canadians, would end up rupturing the national unity that was so dear to him. Laurier figured that supporting the Empire in this way, far from strengthening the Canadian nation, risked destroy-ing it from the inside. Consequently, he considered that it was Eng-lish Canadians' turn to do their part in the historic compromise that he was seeking, and this compromise was to be achieved through a pan-Canadian referendum on this dramatic question. Laurier de-clared peremptorily, and I quote from memory: "If, through a refer-endum, the majority of Canadians say they want conscription, then I will bow to the will of the people." That was Laurier's position in 1917. It was a position that Henri Bourassa heartily endorsed, and this position led finally to the merging of the respective nationalisms of these two public figures.

Gilles Gougeon: But the referendum never happened?

Réal Bélanger: Then the referendum didn't happen — why? Because Robert Laird Borden favoured the kind of imperialist nationalism that counted on conscription at any cost, imposed as soon as possible, to provide further support to the Empire. He believed that conscrip-tion and the remarkable contribution that it would make to the Em-pire's defence represented a faster way for Canada to gain recognition as a full-fledged nation, and he duly minimized the dangers to national unity. Knowing he had the support of the English Canadian majority, Borden rejected the referendum course and chose instead to make a gesture that was unique in the history of Confederation. He formed a Union government composed of Liberals and Conservatives who were in favour of conscription, a government whose aim was quite simple: to do everything possible to achieve conscription for overseas service. Formed on October 12, 1917, this government included two French Canadian Conservatives from Quebec, Albert Sévigny and Pierre-Édouard Blondin. Life for them in Quebec was not going to be easy from that day on.

Gilles Gougeon: What was the role of conscription in Quebec's nationalist affirmation?

Réal Bélanger: Conscription played a very large part, I can tell you. With conscription, the tensions between English Canada and Quebec reached a climax. As I was saying, French Canadians wanted to protect their French Canadian nation and their vision of Canada, but this vision was contradicted by the English Canadian majority's vision. Now, with conscription in 1917-18, there was a brutal awakening, the most brutal possible. It was at this point that the two visions of Canada collided with most dramatic force. Many French Canadians now realized how wide a gulf separated them from English Canadians, and how little they had to look forward to in terms of their own future and their place within Canada.

Gilles Gougeon: French Canadians believed in Canada and thought that English Canadians still believed in England?

Réal Bélanger: I'd say so, it seems that way to me. Certainly French Canadians hoped that English Canadians would come to believe as much as they did in their own vision of Canada. But I would stress that fewer and fewer French Canadians thought that would ever happen.

Gilles Gougeon: And the deaths and confrontations that occurred in the streets of Quebec — did they have repercussions?

Réal Bélanger: The events that unfolded in the spring of 1918 certainly had repercussions, given the drama of those terrible days. But I think the major effects and the extremes of tension in Quebec were felt in the summer of 1917, when conscription was debated and then accepted by vote in the House of Commons in Ottawa. Those votes themselves reveal the tremors that shook the country, that literally rent it in two. On one side the French Canadian MPs voted against conscription; on the other side the English Canadian MPs voted for it. But the fierce discussions that took place among federal MPs were only an echo of the harsh, angry and bitter words that were exchanged in Quebec and English Canada. The word "traitor" was increasingly flung around. And in Quebec people were in a frenzied rage against conscription. They cursed it everywhere and on many occasions angry words gave way to violence.

The situation in several regions of the province was alarming as more people realized — and the pathos was acute — how impossibly divided their country was. The historian Desmond Morton, who wrote that the Great War made of Canada two nations, must surely have been thinking of those stifling summer months of 1917. It was during those long and punishing months that French Canadians had to take stock of the fact that the Canada they believed in was going to be very difficult to share with their partners of 1867. I think it's from 1917 onward that we start hearing rumblings of what would become the Francœur proposal, which I'll come to in a minute.

Gilles Gougeon: What was the effect of this political rift on Quebec after the election of 1917, which has been termed the "khaki" election?

Réal Bélanger: First of all let's talk about the federal election of 1917, one of the most important elections in the history of Confederation, which made the rupture of the country down ethnic faultlines so spectacularly concrete. To try to get across what the atmosphere in Quebec was like, where Laurier's Liberals, allied with Bourassa's nationalists, were confronting the Unionist candidates — that is Borden's Union government — let me simply remind you of the words of a contemporary journalist: it was a campaign behind closed doors. The Unionist candidates could barely campaign in Quebec. If they did they were literally endangering their lives, so outraged was the population against anyone who promoted conscription.

In my research I've studied the 1917 election and in particular one of Borden's French Canadian ministers, Albert Sévigny. This candidate lived through some horrific and terrifying moments. The only political meeting he tried to hold in his Dorchester riding took a tragic turn and he was nearly killed when the crowd's rage went wild.

Attempts to poison him to death and stone-throwing attacks on his home added to his tragedy. This man lived through some unbelievably difficult times, and he wasn't the only Unionist candidate to suffer this way. Everywhere in Quebec, French Canadians were angry and took ferocious exception to anyone who opposed their saviour, Laurier.

What else can I say about the 1917 election, except that it shows French Canadians once again isolated within Canadian Confederation? In Quebec, French Canadians elected sixty-two Liberals out of sixty-five seats, which left only three Unionist MPs, all of whom were elected in Anglophone ridings. In English Canada, Borden had 150 seats against Laurier's twenty — the Liberals were beaten hands down. Never since the time of Lord Durham had Canada been so divided along cultural lines. Henri Bourassa concluded that no French Canadian should take a place in Borden's cabinet, nor therefore in the government of Canada.

It was at this point that the famous Francœur motion was put forward, which was an expression of French Canadians' bitterness. Joseph-Napoléon Francœur was the member of the Quebec Legislative Assembly for the riding of Lotbinière. Exasperated by the attitude of English Canadians and dumbfounded by the results of the last federal election, he announced to the Legislative Assembly on December 21, 1917, the tabling of a bill that went more or less as follows: If English Canadians feel that French Canadians have become an obstacle to the country's development, "This house is of the opinion that the Province of Quebec is prepared to break off the federal pact of 1867." This was quite clearly a separatist-leaning motion, and yet it originated from the Liberal ranks of Premier Lomer Gouin. The motion was debated in the Legislative Assembly starting January 17, 1918, but it was withdrawn by its author before the members could vote on it. So the motion didn't get very far in these federalist parliamentary circles, and it remained more of a symbolic gesture. But it created quite a stir at the time. It allowed for the venting of all the tension that had accumulated over the past months. It permitted a full-blown expression of French Canadian resentment and the depth of the chasm that separated the two nations and their respective nationalist visions. What lay behind the Francœur motion, Mr. Gougeon, was everything I've been talking about this afternoon: the struggles of 1885, 1890, 1896, 1899, 1910, 1912 and 1917 — struggles that French Canadian Catholics had fought in vain. It was from this date that the withdrawal of French

Canadians into the fortress of Quebec really began, it was from there that they would henceforth get on with defending the French Canadian nation.

Gilles Gougeon: How would you define the nationalism that you've been describing to us, from the time of Tardivel until the 1920s? How would you characterize nationalism in French Canada?

Réal Bélanger: Let me first get one thing straight — there was no single kind of French Canadian nationalism during this long period, but many kinds, which together made up the history of nationalism in French Canada.

What were its principal forms? To sum up, the kind of nationalism that was around in 1867 was both political and cultural. It was a nationalism based on collaboration with the English Canadian majority. It was prepared to make compromises as suggested by politicians, who were defending the characteristics of the newly created Canadian nation as well as those of the French Canadian nation, which at times espoused a conservative social ideology and at times a more liberal one. This form of nationalism lasted throughout the period we're interested in here, taking on different guises. Sometimes it would endorse characteristics specific to Canada or to Quebec. Sometimes it would endorse some sort of definition of the two nations. At other times it would endorse something else again. While this multifaceted nationalism had its successes, it also suffered a series of failures over the years that were so discouraging that in the end leaders of the various factions were united, at least in their disillusionment over the reactions of their English Canadian partners. Public figures such as Wilfrid Laurier and Henri Bourassa, who were so divided at some levels but were nonetheless both at the heart of this manifold nationalism, were very disenchanted by 1918.

Another kind of nationalism grew up alongside the kind we've been discussing, a cultural and conservative variety that lasted throughout this same period. It took various forms, but in general it was engaged in defending the principal national characteristics of French Canadians, to which it added its conservative social ideology. This form of nationalism centred on the survival of the French Canadian nation, but it also kept another aim, the peaceful reconquest of the lost territories of New France, very much in the forefront.

In this interview I've focused mainly on the nationalism of Jules-Paul Tardivel, who made his mark on cultural and conservative nationalism with his ultramontane ideas. But I've also shown how he stood out — by the political proposal that he favoured, namely, the separation of Quebec from the rest of Canada. Tardivel's separatist nationalism was marginal in his own time, but after 1920 it inspired nationalist leaders quite a bit, and they were attracted to a number of his aims.

It's important to acknowledge this reality: the expression of French Canadian nationalism between 1867 and 1920 was made up of a combination of all the aspects of the various kinds of nationalism. I should add that at the close of the years 1917-18, the purely French Canadian nationalisms had precious few solutions left to choose from. In fact they had only one: withdrawal to Quebec. This was where you had to fight if you wanted to defend the French Canadian nation appropriately. The expression of purely French Canadian nationalism would dig itself in there for a long time to come.

Bibliography

Bélanger, Réal. *Wilfrid Laurier: Quand la politique devient passion.* Quebec City and Montreal: Presses de l'Université Laval and Entreprises Radio-Canada, 1987.

———. "Le nationalisme ultramontain: le cas de Jules-Paul Tardivel." In *Les ultramontains canadiens-français,* edited by Nive Voisine and Jean Hamelin, pp. 267-303. Montreal: Boréal Express, 1985.

Levitt, Joseph. *Henri Bourassa and the Golden Calf: The Social Program of the Nationalists of Québec, 1900-1914.* Ottawa: Éditions de l'Université d'Ottawa, 1969.

Neatby, H. Blair. *Laurier and a Liberal Quebec.* Toronto: McClelland and Stewart, 1973.

Savard, Pierre. *Jules-Paul Tardivel. La France et les États-Unis 1851-1905.* Quebec City: Presses de l'Université Laval, 1967.

Séguin, Maurice. *L'idée d'indépendance au Québec: Genèse et historique.* Trois-Rivières: Boréal Express, 1968.

Trofimenkoff, Susan Mann. *The Dream of Nation: A Social and Intellectual History of Quebec.* Toronto: Gage, 1983.

Notes

1. The Lieutenant-Governor dismissed the Mercier government after its decision to grant a subsidy to the contractors building the Baie des Chaleurs railway (Matapedia to Gaspé) was shown to have been related to a kickback to Liberal officials. *–tr.*
2. During the 1980 Quebec referendum campaign, the federal government under Pierre Trudeau promised to renew the Canadian constitution if Quebecers voted No to sovereignty-association. After the No side won, the federal government did introduce constitutional proposals, but ones that were widely seen in Quebec as increasing federal centralization. These proposals resulted in the new repatriated constitution of 1982, which the Quebec government under René Lévesque refused to sign. Proposals to amend the constitution to win Quebec's acceptance of it led to the failed constitutional initiatives of the late 1980s and early 1990s. *–tr.*

Part Three

In the third program, we discover how, between 1920 and 1960, the *"Canadiens"* became "French Canadians," confining themselves to Quebec to survive as a people and a nation. During the Great Depression, under the inspiration of Lionel Groulx, they sought to make their presence felt by trying to find a third way between capitalism and socialism. Under Premier Maurice Duplessis, Quebec learned to say no to an increasingly centralist federal government in Ottawa. During the Second World War, conscription breathed new life into the old nationalist demons, which had outgrowths that tended towards fascism.

The historians interviewed are Pierre Trépanier, Robert Comeau and Richard Desrosiers.

Interview with
Pierre Trépanier

Gilles Gougeon: Mr. Trépanier, if you don't mind, I would like you to comment first on the significance that Canon Groulx[1] attached to youth. He seems to have aimed most of his writings and speeches at youth. What was the significance of youth for Canon Groulx?

Pierre Trépanier: Canon Groulx's goal was to put forward a clear nationalist doctrine as a beacon for action that would serve the nation. This quest very quickly led him to the question of politics. But he came to the question of politics in his own particular way — as an educator and moralist. For him, politics was first and foremost a question of people. The quality of the people was more important than constitutional structures or political architecture. As a result, he was instinctively drawn to youth. Youth represented hope for renewal, hope for creative action, while people in office, the powers-that-be, represented the conventional, the routine, which in his mind led to decadence.

Gilles Gougeon: But wasn't there already a kind of political mobilization among young people at that time, which could lead one to believe that a degree of renewal was possible? Was it really necessary to whip young people up to interest them in politics, as you say?

Pierre Trépanier: There were youth movements, and Groulx had helped found some of them, such as the Action Catholique de la Jeunesse Canadienne-Française (Catholic Action of French Canadian Youth). There was also the Ligue Nationaliste Canadienne (*Canadien* Nationalist League), whose central figures were Olivar Asselin, a student of his named Fournier, and others. But Groulx wanted to light their way. He wanted to provide them with a doctrine so that they could develop a clear plan before plunging directly into action. Groulx believed that action should be preceded and illuminated by thought and reflection, and he wanted to lead young people along this path.

It's important to understand that in Groulx's conception of things, willpower was central. He believed that people could change their situation. And so he believed that you could change people, and especially leaders, if you knew how to educate them. That was why training a new elite was part of his plan. And to do this, you might as well address youth directly, because that way you were engaging the root of the problem. Groulx wanted to lead French Canada towards showing a little boldness, and a little intellectual consistency. To this end, it seemed easier to speak to youth than to speak to the *notables* who were the leaders of French Canadian society and who, as a group, were a disappointment to him.

Gilles Gougeon: You say that he wanted to train the elite, that he addressed his message to them. How significant was the whole idea of an elite at that time, in the context in which Groulx carried out his social and political action?

Pierre Trépanier: For him, the elite was the engine of society. Almost all the people in his circle — classical college teachers, the clergy in general, and pretty well all the intellectuals of the time — believed that it was the elite that brought about both change and decadence. So your best bet for achieving your goals was in concentrating your efforts on them.

Gilles Gougeon: Groulx was a preacher. He was a priest and he also preached his nationalist message. But he doesn't seem to have had a well articulated political plan. For example, did he have a modern conception of the state? What role did he see the government as playing in the conduct of day-to-day political life?

Pierre Trépanier: Groulx's goal was the national affirmation of French Canadians. Now, one of the ways of achieving this was to train new elites. But the other way — and this may have been Groulx's chief contribution to the debate — lay in his insistence on the role of the state in national affirmation. What did national affirmation mean for Groulx? In a sense, it meant neutralizing the harmful or corrupting effects of the "conquest." And to achieve this neutralization, the state had to be nationalized, so to speak. The provincial state of Quebec had to be put at the service of what Groulx called "French integrity." In brief, French integrity meant a full and rich life for the French Canadian collectivity, instead of the diminished or weakened life to which it had been condemned since the conquest. The state was essential to this program of action. Indeed, one of Groulx's great contributions was to direct his contemporaries' attention to the importance of the state.

Gilles Gougeon: But at that time — okay, today it may be quite hard to understand because the state is omnipresent in our lives. It has crept in everywhere, especially since 1960. But can you describe the role of the state a little for me in this context? Because Groulx wanted to give it a different role. What did the state do at that time? It didn't play an important role, the way it does today.

Pierre Trépanier: No, the state was not involved in all sectors of social life, the way it is today, although from the turn of the century on, the state had been taking more and more initiatives in the area of education and, to a lesser extent, in the social sphere. But the state was not involved in the day-to-day management of society and the economy the way it is today. More government intervention was exactly what Groulx wanted, because he saw the state as a powerful instrument of national affirmation, and the only one French Canadians could count on in terms of public institutions.

Groulx synthesized this idea of serving the nation or promoting national affirmation through the state into a formula. That formula was what Groulx called the "French State." But that raises the question of what Groulx meant by the French State. To the extent that the French State was synonymous with serving the interests of Groulx's concept of French integrity, Groulx's formula never wavered. In this sense, his idea of the French State remained the same throughout his career. He liked to evoke this idea of the French State in his major speeches. But when he tried to specify the concrete constitutional form it should take, he would begin to hesitate. The best way to show this would be to go through the different stages of Groulx's career, but, rather than do that here, I will just summarize it by saying that while he was more receptive to the idea of independence during the 1920s and towards the end of his life,[2] mostly he hoped to be able to build his French State within the framework of Confederation.

Gilles Gougeon: So when he talked about provincial autonomy, he was talking about autonomy within the Confederation framework.

He wasn't against Ottawa; he wasn't against the state as it had existed since 1867.

Pierre Trépanier: He wasn't against Canadian federalism as long as its binational character was respected.

Gilles Gougeon: Groulx knew very well that a French State could not exist on a Canada-wide scale. So did he see a French State — Quebec, to make it clear — that would gradually detach itself or isolate itself from political decisions in the rest of the country, or did he see it developing within Confederation?

Pierre Trépanier: For Groulx, the French State could be achieved within Confederation, so long as two conditions were met. The first was that the Province of Quebec and its government be expansive, audacious and imaginative in exercising all the powers given them by Confederation in 1867. But the other condition was that the English Canadian partners first of all accept this idea of French integrity and make it a central principle in Canada, and then agree to enter into the binational partnership in which Groulx believed. If one or the other of these conditions was missing, then it would be necessary to consider the possibility of building the French State outside Confederation. So from this point of view, Groulx's thinking was close to Henri Bourassa's, to the extent that both envisaged building the French State inside Confederation.

Gilles Gougeon: But Henri Bourassa himself was disappointed at the end of his political life. He no longer believed that French Canada could fulfil itself within Confederation. Did Groulx pick up the torch of hope within the country? How were Groulx's ideas received in the rest of the country?

Pierre Trépanier: Groulx's ideas were very poorly received in English Canada. He was considered an extremist, with all the negative connotations that go along with that term. Some people even considered him a racist. Groulx was not heard in the rest of Canada. His message didn't go over. It went over among French Canadians, especially young people and some politicians, but even there he spoke to a minority. Groulx was a kind of prophet, if you will, someone who roused and enlivened people, but you can't say he had huge contingents of the population behind him. His immediate influence was more limited. And in English Canada he met with rejection.

Gilles Gougeon: Let's talk a bit about his being a priest. Today it's hard to imagine someone linking religion, language and the state so closely. What was the significance of Catholicism, of the Christian faith, in Groulx's nationalist activity?

Pierre Trépanier: This is one of the keys for understanding Groulx. We have to remember that Groulx was not only a believer but also a priest. First of all, he paid attention to the religious dimension as a sociologist and as a historian. He recognized that French Canada's origins were tied up with France and the Catholic Church. But these sociological or historical conclusions didn't begin to exhaust the reality of religion for Groulx. Religion, for him, was the highest value: it ranked at the top of his scale of values. Religion was more than simply one factor among others — Groulx was convinced that God was the master of history. Religion illuminated everything else; it was the norm, in a way; and it served as the measuring stick for his nationalism. Groulx always wanted to situate his nationalism within Catholic orthodoxy. He tried to define his thinking in relation to papal teaching and he tried to keep it within the bounds of orthodoxy.

Religion also had another significance in Groulx's thinking: it developed into the idea of the mission of French Canada. Groulx didn't invent this idea of mission. It was passed on to him by his teachers, so to speak: the intellectuals who came before him. But of all our intellectuals, he may have been the one who expressed it with the most conviction and made it a particularly seductive ideal for believing minds like his own.

Gilles Gougeon: A word about Groulx's economic nationalism, because even though he was a priest and a historian he was very interested in economics. He even taught at the École des Hautes Études Commerciales in Montreal. What significance did he attach to economics and economic nationalism?

Pierre Trépanier: I've said that Groulx's nationalism had a religious dimension, a spiritual dimension, but it wasn't a disembodied nationalism. Quite the contrary. Of all the nationalists of his time, Groulx was among those who best understood the importance of the economy, the importance of material factors, not only for national affirmation but also for Catholic mission. The minimum conditions for economic prosperity had to be met so that the French Canadian nation could flourish and fulfil its role. So Groulx saw the economic question in terms of undertaking a reconquest — the reconquest of the French Canadian economy. As he witnessed the massive and rapid urbanization of French Canada taking place at the time, Groulx was absolutely horrified to see French Canada sink into proletarianization. And under the prevailing conditions, French Canada could become urbanized and industrialized only at the cost of becoming proletarianized.

So his program of economic reconquest bore some resemblance to his program of political self-assertion. Part of it involved training people, which meant developing skills. That's why he wanted to see progress in education, especially higher scientific, technical and commercial education. He considered it important to have a class of French Canadian entrepreneurs, bold entrepreneurs who not only were interested in succeeding individually in business but who would also, as they prospered, remain patriots and therefore continue to contribute to national affirmation.

He was also counting on the state, because the forces against which French Canadians had to fight were extremely powerful. They were the forces of big capital, whether English Canadian, British or — increasingly — American. So he was counting on the state to coordinate action, or rather, to coordinate a reaction against this massive presence of capitalism, especially American capitalism. In his mind, this didn't mean that the government should plunge into a huge program of nationalization. Lionel Groulx wasn't a socialist — far from it. He was a supporter of private property and private initiative. But in some sectors, such as hydroelectricity, he saw room for government intervention, which in some cases could go as far as nationalization. He saw the role of the state as primarily that of a coordinator, a guide. He also saw government intervention in terms of the state's responsibility to look out for the overall smooth running of society. This meant controls on foreign capital where necessary. It also meant bringing some kind of morality into industrial life and factory work. Thus, social concerns rounded out Groulx's economic program.

Gilles Gougeon: Today he would have been more of a social democrat, we would say.

Pierre Trépanier: No, I wouldn't say that he would have been a social democrat, because individual responsibility was too crucial to his system of thought for him to be firmly on the side of social democracy. Groulx always remained attached to a fundamental idea, what's called the social doctrine of the Church, and to the principle of subsidiarity that is at the heart of that idea. This means that responsibilities have to be left to lower levels of society. Individuals, families, organizations and regions have to assume their responsibilities. The state should take charge only of those tasks that lower levels can't assume on their own, so its function would be helping or filling in for these lower levels. Social democracy, as we know it today, depends too much on government intervention, even on a day-to-day basis, for the idea of subsidiarity to be able to coexist with the social democratic state. So I don't think Groulx would have gone that far.

Gilles Gougeon: You've pointed out the importance that Groulx attached to religion, to faith. How did he react to the first signs of the Quiet Revolution, when faith and the structures of the Church within Quebec society were called into question?

Pierre Trépanier: It is precisely the importance that Groulx attached to religion that explains his ambivalence towards the Quiet Revolution. On the one hand, he was very happy about the national affirmation inherent in the Quiet Revolution. In this regard, Groulx could only congratulate himself on seeing part of his program come to pass before his eyes. On the other hand, there was another side to the Quiet Revolution that he would have called collective apostasy — that is, secularization or the loss of society's religious character. This was a genuine tragedy for him. At the end of his life, he seemed to be tortured by this aspect of the Quiet Revolution, because he saw French Canada as losing something essential.

We have to remember that in his definition of French Canada, in his conception of the French Canadian identity, French Canada was both French and Catholic. So it seemed to him that a whole side of the French Canadian identity was sold off without a second thought, in return for values that he considered materialist and therefore foreign to his conception of things and to his conception of history, as he had taught it throughout his long career at the University of Montreal.

Gilles Gougeon: Groulx had a sense of the state, of the nation. How would you gauge the idea of the nation at the time when Groulx began to talk about it? What was the nation for Groulx?

Pierre Trépanier: For Groulx, the nation was essentially a historical community based on culture. Groulx never believed that national characteristics — at least the important ones, the ones that served as the foundation for his concept of "French integrity" that I spoke of earlier — could be transmitted through blood. So Groulx did not have a racial conception of the nation. Nor did Groulx espouse the racist ideas that were becoming fashionable in Europe in the thirties. Groulx never believed in genetically fixed racial superiority.

But he did believe, like most people of his generation, that some civilizations were superior to others. Not races — civilizations. But it was a superiority based on effort, on merit, and also on the material resources available to a particular civilization. In this respect, Groulx could say that eighteenth-century France represented a higher civilization than, say, Iroquois civilization. But it was a precarious superiority, constantly stalked by the possibility of decadence. Groulx was acutely aware that nations and civilizations were mortal. Superiority, for him, was always *de facto* superiority, not superiority by right. It was always a temporary superiority, a superiority that had to be maintained, and not a superiority given once and for all through birth, genetic inheritance and blood. In this sense, Groulx was really not a racist.

Gilles Gougeon: But at the time, Groulx spoke of the French Canadian race. What did the word "race" signify at the time?

Pierre Trépanier: The word "race" appears very frequently in Groulx's writings and speeches, as it does in the language of almost all his contemporaries. At the time, the word "race" simply meant "nation, nationality, ethnic group, cultural community."

To understand Groulx, there's another fact that has to be taken into account, and that is that he was a lover of literature. He had a deliberately declamatory style. His reading had instilled a certain vocabulary in him; he was, for example, a great admirer of Barrès.[3] So for literary effect, he could be more inclined to use the word "race" than terms that might seem more technical, such as ethnic group or nation. It's not that he wasn't aware of these terms, but he spoke the way people in most French Canadian circles spoke in his time.

Gilles Gougeon: You say that Groulx was not a racist. However, now when we read his writings of the time, when he talks about Jews, when he talks about blood, when he talks about his fear of mixed marriages between Anglophones and Francophones, we can see arguments there that are racist in character. How should we interpret these arguments if he was not a racist?

Pierre Trépanier: To answer that question, I think we first have to define what anti-Semitism is, because I suppose when someone uses the term anti-Semitism, they use it in the sense it has acquired in the twentieth century — that is, as a form of racism. And right away the image of Nazi Germany comes to mind. That is what I would call doctrinal anti-Semitism, an ideological system in which anti-Semitism occupies an absolutely central place. This vision of the world, this reading of history, is structured around anti-Semitism. If you take anti-Semitism out of this ideological system, the system could crumble.

With Groulx, you find criticisms and warnings about some Jews and some Jewish institutions. But these criticisms and warnings are not frequent and occupy a very small place in the mass of his writings. They are peripheral; they are secondary and marginal in relation to what he says. In consequence, it can't be said that Groulx was a doctrinal anti-Semite.

In his time, in the late 1920s and the 1930s, people in French Canada believed, rightly or wrongly, that the increasing presence of Jews in Montreal could threaten French Canadian small retailing and small business. Groulx attracted the attention of French Canadians to this problem and even, in a sense, offered the Jewish community as an example to French Canadians in inviting them to practise economic solidarity as well. But I don't think that's enough to make him a racist anti-Semite. Making allowances for the difference in scale, his attitude towards Jews in economic terms was more or less the same attitude he had towards American capitalism. It was an essentially defensive reaction.

Now we could look at the problem from another angle and ask whether Groulx was an anti-Semitic *historian*. Here the answer is clearly no, and it's a categorical no because Groulx does not mention the Jews in his historical writings. You find them in his polemical writings — in his political writings, if you like — but not in his historical writings. In his historical works, Groulx wrote about the French, the English, the Americans, the Canadians and God, because God was a character in Groulx's history, as he conceived of it. But he didn't talk about the Jews. So you can't say that Groulx was an anti-Semitic historian.

There is one final aspect that needs to be addressed: what I would call anti-Judaism. And this aspect was connected with religion for Groulx. Traditionally, in Christian countries, there was a mistrust of Jews. It was a mutual mistrust: Christian mistrust of Jews and Jewish mistrust of Christians. This mistrust flows from a basic doctrinal opposition; only someone who isn't on either side can see this opposition as a simple difference of opinion. But for the Christian believer, on one side, and the Jewish believer, on the other, it isn't a simple difference of opinion — it's really something fundamental. And this difference has to do with the messiah, with Jesus Christ. So a whole psychological and cultural complex of mistrust towards Jews grew up out of this opposition on a fundamental fact of sacred history. Groulx was influenced by his education and by his Catholic culture, and in his writings you can find some traces of this traditional mistrust of Jews. But this wasn't anti-Semitism in the twentieth-century sense, that is racist anti-Semitism.

Gilles Gougeon: In conclusion, if I asked you to place Groulx in the whole history of the development of nationalism, from the end of the French Regime to our own time, how would you characterize the role that he played in this history of Quebec, of French Canada? What was he for you?

Pierre Trépanier: I would say that among the major thinkers, it was Groulx who had the clearest view of the role of the state in national affirmation. In this sense, Groulx's nationalism was notably modern, much more modern than Henri Bourassa's — especially since he didn't have the same sentimental attachment to Confederation that Bourassa had. You could say that Groulx's attachment to Canada was an attachment of convenience, while his attachment to French Canada was one of genuine passion, so he concentrated his efforts on French Canada and especially on the French Canada of the St. Lawrence region, the territory of Quebec. That led him to define the nation better than his predecessors had, not only in relation to its cultural roots but also in relation to the physical country, specifically the territory of Quebec, and to the political institutions that French Canadians had built in this territory of Quebec. And in this sense, his conception of national affirmation and the nation was modern, because he integrated political and territorial factors better than his predecessors had.

Bibliography

Frégault, Guy. *Lionel Groulx tel qu'en lui-même*. Montreal: Leméac, 1978.

Gaboury, Jean-Pierre. *Le nationalisme de Lionel Groulx: Aspects idéologiques*. Ottawa: Éditions de l'Université d'Ottawa, 1970.

"Lionel Groulx, 1878-1978, 100e anniversaire de sa naissance." *Revue d'histoire de l'Amérique française* 32, no. 3 (December 1978), special issue.

Robert, Jean-Claude. *Du Canada français au Québec libre*. Paris: Flammarion, 1975.

Trofimenkoff, Susan Mann. *Action Française: French Canadian Nationalism in Quebec in the Twenties*. Toronto: University of Toronto Press, 1975.

Notes

1. Lionel Groulx was a priest who held the ecclesiastical titles of *Chanoine* (Canon) and *Abbé*, and hence is often referred to as either "Canon Groulx" or "Abbé Groulx." –*tr*.
2. Groulx died in 1967. –*tr*.
3. Maurice Barrès (1862-1923) was a writer of the nationalist and traditionalist school in France. –*tr*.

Interview with
Robert Comeau (i)

Gilles Gougeon: Mr. Comeau, I'd like to talk first about the 1930s. How would you characterize the Quebec nationalism of those years?

Robert Comeau: During the Great Depression, nationalism was revitalized. There was a radicalization of Quebec nationalism, which took a number of forms. The dominant current was not separatist; rather, it favoured autonomy and was linked with very conservative socioeconomic ideas, inspired by the corporatist ideal as practised in southern Europe, especially in Salazar's Portugal.[1] Around 1935, there even appeared an extreme-right-wing separatist faction, sympathetic to fascism and fiercely anti-communist. The main tendency was more moderately autonomist and conservative, although the corporatist ideal was very seductive to the Quebec intelligentsia of the period.

Gilles Gougeon: But when you're a conservative, it means you're protecting yourself, you're afraid. What were people afraid of? How do you explain the fact that this nationalism was so conservative?

Robert Comeau: In response to the deterioration of living conditions, a strong movement emerged that attacked the "dictatorship of monopolies" at the root of the Depression. People challenged the established disorder, and liberalism and liberal democracy were called into question. This challenge came both from the left (socialists and communists) and from the right — supporters of the "third way" challenged the established order just as ferociously.

These people said they were fighting both the dictatorship of monopolies and communism. Corporatism, which they presented as the third way, wasn't really anti-capitalist but was simply a rejection of powerful foreign capitalists. The nationalist right didn't question the foundations of private ownership. It challenged the constitutional regime and foreign political and economic domination. It denounced the federalist political elites' inability to find a solution to unemployment, accusing them of treason.

The more radical ideas were mostly expressed by a nationalist wing that took its inspiration in large part from Abbé Groulx and the social program of the Jesuits of the École Sociale Populaire. Groulx's disciples built a virtual cult around him. This "national leader" encouraged the young French Canadian nationalists and separatists who were involved in groups such as the Jeunesses Patriotes (Patriotic Youth) or the newspaper *La Nation*. In Quebec, as in the rest of Canada, there were manifestations of intolerance and racism. This development wasn't foreign to Quebec, but it wasn't unique to Quebec either. The same ideological polarization occurred in English Canada.

Gilles Gougeon: Was there much interest in people like Adrien Arcand and his group? Was this a marginal phenomenon or was it fairly significant at the time?

Robert Comeau: In my view, this was not the group that attracted the most supporters in Quebec. Adrien Arcand, who was pro-Hitler, founded a federalist party that advocated Canadian unity and an alliance of Catholics and Protestants against the Jews. Groulx and most French Canadian nationalists were more favourable to the fascist ideas of Mussolini, Salazar and Franco, whom they called the "Latins." Even Paul Bouchard, the fascist and corporatist separatist leader, was opposed to the federalist Arcand. There were more pro-Nazi groups in English Canada, especially in Ontario, in Toronto.

Gilles Gougeon: How do you explain the fact that the ideas and ideals of Franco, Salazar and Mussolini were so successful at the time?

Robert Comeau: It's important to understand that these countries seemed to have found a solution to unemployment, to the Depression — through highway construction, for example, and through the armaments industry. Since parliamentary debates seemed ineffective in dealing with the Depression, people wanted a more interventionist government and more authoritarian leaders. At last they saw a new model being put forward that was opposed to the communist model. In the right-wing current in Quebec that was influenced by the church, "mediating bodies" — Catholic pressure groups — were supposed to play an important role. This current used the socialist model as a foil. Under the church's influence, people rejected communism and tried to find a third way between that model and a discredited liberalism. There was a revolt among intellectuals, a deep unease, a questioning of the ideology of laissez-faire and monopoly capitalism. In a kind of pseudo–anti-capitalism, nationalists borrowed the anti-trust rhetoric of the far left. For example, in 1934 the young nationalist Guy Frégault adopted slogans about the need for French-speaking fascists to carry out a "national revolution."

Corporatism, this pseudo–third way, had a great influence on nationalist, political, religious and even trade union elites in the years before the Second World War. Abbé Groulx[2] and economists such as François-Albert Angers flirted with the corporatist ideal, which was a reactionary ideal in the sense that it advocated an unattainable return to the guilds of the Middle Ages, when there was no class conflict between master craftsman and apprentice. This ideal of a consensus society, which denied the existence of opposing interests and antagonistic classes, was utopian. It wasn't even applied in Italy.

Gilles Gougeon: Let's focus on what was happening in Canada at the time. Was Canadian nationalism alive at the time, in the thirties, and how did these right-wing ideas show up in Canada?

Robert Comeau: In English Canada, and especially in Toronto, there were organizations and movements that were openly fascist. There was a Canadian nationalist party as well, and it, too, was on the far right. In Quebec you don't hear about the existence of these groups very often, but they were much better organized and had a lot more members than Adrien Arcand's organization in Montreal.

There were demonstrations of xenophobia and racism in Toronto, and the people who were in charge of the Department of Immigration at the time made it very difficult for German Jews to enter Canada. And it was not Francophones who were running the department! There were avowed anti-Semites at the head of the Department of Immigration. I'm thinking of O.D. Skelton in particular, but there were several others as well. In the period before the Second World War, even members of the Mackenzie King government had sympathy for Hitler; they found him very attractive. We've largely forgotten that period before the Second World War. In Ontario, there were many instances of repression of Jews or other nationalities. It's repeated over and over again that it was only in Quebec that these forms of xenophobia showed up, and I think it has to be said that this was not so.

Gilles Gougeon: Did this xenophobia also exist outside Ontario, in the western provinces?

Robert Comeau: In the West as well. For example, there was the repression of the Japanese who were put in camps and interned during this period, or if you go back a bit further in time, there was the repression of the Chinese who came to work for the railway companies. There was very strong repression, along with mistrust and racism. This doesn't mean we can say that all English Canadians are racists, but there were racist groups in English Canada as well. For example, the first Ku Klux Klan groups were not founded in Quebec. There had been such groups in English Canada for fifty years. Another example is the Orange Order in Ontario, which was anti-Catholic and anti-Francophone and had fought French Canadians from the nineteenth century on. From that point of view, there was a lot of racism and xenophobia in Canada in the 1930s. Not primarily in Quebec, but everywhere, in all the provinces of Canada.

Bibliography

Anctil, Pierre. *"Le Devoir," les Juifs et l'immigration: De Bourassa à Laurendeau.* Quebec City: Institut Québécois de Recherche sur la Culture, 1988.

Comeau, Robert. "Les indépendantistes de 'La Nation' 1936-1938." Master's thesis, University of Montreal, 1971.

Notes

1. Corporatism envisaged a harmonious society based on "corporations" similar to the guilds of the Middle Ages, and was an element of the ideology of a number of authoritarian regimes in Europe before the Second World War. António de Oliveira Salazar (1889-1970) was dictator of Portugal from 1932 to 1968. – *tr.*
2. See note 1, page 65.

Interview with
Richard Desrosiers (i)

Gilles Gougeon: Mr. Desrosiers, I would like to begin by trying to understand what Maurice Duplessis's intentions were when he entered politics in the early 1930s. How did this man make his appearance in the history of Quebec nationalism?

Richard Desrosiers: Duplessis first stood out as an adroit politician. The mid-1930s was a time not only of economic crisis but of political crisis as well — the Liberal government of Louis-Alexandre Taschereau was really at the end of its rope and there were a lot of free-floating political forces. Now Duplessis, who had been leader of the Quebec Conservative Party since 1933, managed to bring a number of these political forces together: the Conservatives, nationalists, and the Action Libérale Nationale, made up of dissident Liberals. It seemed that this new grouping might be able to find a solution to the Depression and offer a path towards change. Some people have even said that a quiet revolution was in the air in Quebec at the time, but that's a gross exaggeration because Maurice Duplessis was first and foremost a conservative.

But as an adroit politician, he got his message across and represented an alternative to a corrupt Liberal government — after fifteen years in power, Taschereau was really tired. Nationalism wasn't a major theme for Duplessis at the beginning, although it was for the people who were challenging the system in the 1930s: they demanded the nationalization of electricity. Duplessis would say, "Yes, yes, I agree with you," when he was still the lawyer for Shawinigan Water and Power![1]

Duplessis brought together the different fragments of the opposition and formed the Union Nationale. The way he co-opted them was fantastic. He created a new party by bringing together old Conservatives, nationalists and dissident Liberals. And that's how he took centre stage. At a time of political and economic crisis, a crisis of confidence in the incumbent government, he took centre stage and came to power. But in 1936, he was not very nationalist himself, even though he had nationalist elements in his party. It was only later, in

1944, that Duplessis would understand the importance of playing the nationalist card, the autonomy card.

Gilles Gougeon: When we think of the creation of the Union Nationale at the time, surely we have to think of it as a fairly new political phenomenon.

Richard Desrosiers: Yes, because it was the first political party that was frankly a Quebec party. There had been the Honoré Mercier episode:[2] in the political atmosphere created by the Riel affair, Honoré Mercier had managed to bring together Conservatives and Liberals, but this alliance lasted only as long as the situation that created it. Once the crisis was over and Mercier was gone, it was back to the two good old parties. And the Conservatives, like the provincial Liberals, remained members of a major federal party.

Gilles Gougeon: There were no provincial parties at the time?

Richard Desrosiers: No. Even in the case of the Quebec provincial Liberals, it was not until 1955 that Georges-Émile Lapalme would establish a federation, a kind of autonomous grouping within the larger Liberal Party of Canada, and not until the early sixties that the Quebec Liberal Party would be established. Now Duplessis established the Union Nationale, a party without federal ties, as early as 1936. It was the first real political party that was deeply Québécois — quite a coup! And to do it with the old Conservatives! Note that the provincial Conservatives disappeared at the same time, as did the Action Libérale Nationale — which you could say was the first Quebec party, but it was short-lived. The Action Libérale Nationale lasted through the 1935 election, and then was co-opted by the Union Nationale. And the Union Nationale took centre stage, with no federal big brother. From that point of view, Duplessis had the merit of creating something new with the Union Nationale.

Gilles Gougeon: At this time, during the 1930s — in 1935, 1938 — what forms did Quebec nationalism take?

Richard Desrosiers: Canon Groulx[3] was very influential. It was a conservative form of nationalism, what has been called traditional nationalism, in which values of faith and language were very important, along with our traditions, our history — *notre maître le passé* (our master the past), as Canon Groulx said. *Survivance* (survival) was still a major theme. And Duplessis was a faithful representative of the dominant nationalist rhetoric, which he adopted without really adding anything to it. "Our government is a good government because it is Catholic and French" was something he picked up.

He talked about traditions, about the importance of conserving our heritage, about values of authority and family. Even about the land: Duplessis could pull out plenty of "agriculturalist" rhetoric to show that he adhered to the conservative values of the time, which saw the clergy as influential and religion as important. In this sense, the nationalist rhetoric of the 1930s was conservative rhetoric, rhetoric based on the past, on ideas of *survivance*. The idea was that providence put us here to spread the Catholic faith: this was our main role, our mission. These weren't new things, but Duplessis was a perfect representative — the last one — of traditional conservative nationalism. I say he was the last because by the late 1950s this kind of nationalism had run out of steam.

Duplessis kept up the same rhetoric through the thirties, forties and fifties, with the difference that after 1944 he added the idea of provincial autonomy. He wasn't an autonomist in the true sense of the word. On constitutional questions, Duplessis believed in 1867, he believed in federalism, and you would be mistaken to think that Duplessis was a separatist — he wasn't at all! On the contrary, the few times he mentioned separatism, it was with disdain, disgust, contempt. Duplessis believed in 1867, Canadian Confederation, the Confederation pact. It was a good thing for Quebecers, for the province, according to his definition of nationalism, based on tradition, faith and language.

Gilles Gougeon: But if Duplessis believed in 1867-style federalism, how do you explain the fact that he attacked Ottawa so much?

Richard Desrosiers: According to him, it was Ottawa that changed the rules of the game, especially during and after the Second World War. Duplessis thought that Canadian Confederation was threatened by Ottawa's centralist designs. And he was partly right. He was right in the sense that starting with the Second World War, Ottawa understood how the federal state had to develop: intervention in the economy, social policy — in short, the welfare state. The federal Liberals understood Keynesianism, they understood the New Deal, and they took the lead in creating a more modern state. In the forties and fifties, the federal government's budget increased tenfold, twenty-fold. It was fantastic!

Ottawa was aggressive, and the provinces more or less went along. During the war they agreed to let go of the provincial income tax. Then they allowed the federal government to establish various social measures, like old age pensions and family allowances. In the fifties, even a universal hospital insurance plan was favourably received by the other nine Canadian provinces. But when it came to Quebec, the rise of the Canadian welfare state ran up against provincial autonomy. After all, social policy, cultural policy, education — these are all under provincial jurisdiction. A federal hospital insurance plan makes no sense in terms of 1867. So Duplessis was right to attack these centralizing initiatives.

But Ottawa didn't want to centralize for the pure pleasure of centralizing, even though some people came to that conclusion. It was not out of anti-Quebec sentiment that Ottawa acted in this way, but because it wanted to create a modern welfare state. To do this, it was, well, "obliged" to invade fields of provincial jurisdiction. That is why Duplessis stood on guard, speaking out in defence of *"notre butin"* (what belongs to us): only the provinces had the right to be concerned with social policy! It was the responsibility of religious communities to take care of health and education. All this could lead us to think that Duplessis resisted Ottawa and favoured autonomy out of conservatism and not just out of nationalism. Because we know, in any case, that Duplessis — staunch conservative that he was — didn't like the increased role of the state in social policy and education.

Gilles Gougeon: What did Duplessis say no to?

Richard Desrosiers: Before I answer, I would like to phrase the question in a different way. Duplessis was enormously afraid of the increasing economic and social role of the state. He feared the establishment of a hospital insurance plan and a department of education in Quebec. He was against these things, politically and ideologically.

Gilles Gougeon: Why?

Richard Desrosiers: Why had the entire elite feared the state since the middle of the nineteenth century, since the failure of the Patriotes? Both because of the church, which permeated everything and was the driving force behind this repugnance that politicians had developed towards the state, and because people didn't yet see that you could make progress by relying on the collectivity. It was only later that nationalists would discover this. So Duplessis did not invent this traditional way of seeing things.

Pierre Elliott Trudeau and his colleagues at *Cité Libre* were right, up to a point, when they equated Duplessis's nationalism with his conservatism. It was true that Duplessis resisted Ottawa as much out of nationalism as out of conservatism — up to that point they were right. But to go from that to thinking that all nationalism is conservative — that's where I think *Cité Libre* and Pierre Elliott Trudeau were wrong. But that's another question.

To get back to Duplessis, he didn't want to see the state invade the social field, the economic field, et cetera. Since the federal government took the initiative in these fields, he said no, no, no. But with hindsight, we realize — and here I'm getting back to your question — what he was saying no to: no to family allowances, no to unemployment insurance. Fortunately, Duplessis was in opposition for a while, from 1939 to 1944, or I don't know what would have happened.

No to a hospital insurance plan. During the 1950s, Quebecers didn't benefit from this program, unlike other Canadian citizens, and yet they were paying taxes for it just the same. The first measure the Lesage government[4] would take was to establish a Quebec hospital insurance plan.

No to a rental board. No to the construction of the Trans-Canada Highway — but that may have been to protect the favouritism practised by the Union Nationale. And finally, no to federal grants to universities. Whenever the federal government took an initiative, the Duplessis government said no. But it was negative in the sense that there was never a Quebec counterpart. It wasn't, "No to federal grants to universities, but I'm going to give more money to the universities." He didn't give money to the universities. "No to a federal hospital insurance plan, but I'm establishing a Quebec plan." He never established one because he didn't want one. He didn't believe in government measures or initiatives of this kind.

That is why nationalists, who at the beginning saw him as a kindred spirit, with hindsight ended up saying "*Ma foi*, all he ever did was say no." Thus *Le Devoir* was squeezed between supporting nationalism and opposing Duplessis's social policies — for example, the newspaper supported the strikers at Asbestos.[5] Like the nationalists of the Montreal Saint-Jean-Baptiste Society, *Le Devoir* was slow to understand that Duplessis was nationalist, to be sure, but didn't contribute towards building anything concrete for Quebec. Duplessis said no.

Now Lesage never wanted to call himself an autonomist and thought of himself as deeply federalist — if you had said to him "You're an autonomist like Mr. Duplessis," he would have flatly denied it. But in fact he was more autonomist than Duplessis ever was. Lesage brought us a Quebec hospital insurance plan, he brought us a Quebec pension plan, he recovered tax points, et cetera.

Gilles Gougeon: At the beginning, when Duplessis took power, there was a great feeling of liberation; people said "Good, we're rid of Taschereau and the Liberal Party's corruption." Then the Liberals came to power again during the war. Let's go back to this period of the war, the period of conscription. In 1942 there was a plebiscite, and in this brouhaha, nationalists emerged. So how should we see the part played by nationalism in the 1942 plebiscite?

Richard Desrosiers: The nationalists of the thirties — they were all over the place, in the Action Libérale Nationale, in the fight against the trusts,[6] finally in the Union Nationale — were people whose demands were for more repatriation on the constitutional level, and more measures that would make French Canadians *"Maîtres chez nous,"* Masters in our own house, on the economic level. Think of the struggle against the trusts waged by Dr. Philippe Hamel, who wanted to see electricity nationalized. These people were more or less co-opted by the Union Nationale. At the beginning, when Duplessis took power in 1936, people weren't aware of that. It was after a year or two that they realized that Duplessis was just a clever politician and their dream of change would not come true. So at the very beginning of the war, the nationalists were in a state of great disappointment. For them, the Bloc Populaire represented a second wind, a new base around which to organize, from which they could take off and actually defend the Quebec nation.

Duplessis lost the 1939 election, largely because the federal Liberals engaged in a kind of blackmail by saying "If you don't elect Liberals in Quebec City, we, the federal Liberals, won't guarantee that we will protect you against the possible imposition of conscription." During the First World War, conscription had been imposed in 1917. An election divided the country at the time. The army had to intervene in Quebec to force conscripts to go. The image that Quebecers had of conscription could not have been more negative. It was a measure imposed by the federal government. Besides, the army was a means of Anglicizing Quebecers, and Francophone Quebecers were the first to be sent to the front lines during the war. In short, conscription — people didn't want it.

I'm sure that the blackmail was effective. Ernest Lapointe, the federal minister of justice under Mackenzie King, came to campaign for the provincial Liberals. In effect, it was Ernest Lapointe and not Adélard Godbout[7] who led the Liberals and was in charge of the campaign. So Duplessis was on the defensive. Duplessis was afraid of the war. He had to censor his speeches on the radio because Canada was at war. In addition, Duplessis was an alcoholic at the time, which complicated his personal management of his political life. To make a long story short, Duplessis lost the election. Even though they had had barely three years of the Union Nationale government, I think Quebecers bet on the Liberals again to avoid conscription.

Now, a few years later, the federal government realized that there weren't enough men, there weren't enough combat troops, there weren't enough soldiers. That was why Mackenzie King imposed the plebiscite in 1942. In 1939, a formal promise had been made to Quebecers: no conscription, we'll protect you against conscription if you elect a Liberal provincial government, which Quebecers did. The federal government knew it had made that promise; hence the plebiscite. Look at how subtle the question was: "Do you consent to liberate the government from any obligation arising from prior engagements restraining the methods of mobilization for military service?" This engagement was made to Quebecers alone. The referendum, on the other hand, was Canada-wide.

The organization for a "no" to conscription, a "no" in the referendum, brought together all the nationalists of the thirties, including supporters of the Union Nationale. Duplessis played a very delicate role here. He didn't want to get directly involved in the fight against conscription. In 1942 the plebiscite was held, and in Canada as a whole, a bit more than 60 per cent of the population said yes. But if you look at the figures, 80 per cent said no in Quebec and 80 per cent said yes in the rest of Canada. That's why there was a majority for the yes side. But in fact, Quebec said no. What got people pissed off — excuse the expression — was that it was English Canada that released the government from the promise it had made to Quebec not to impose conscription. Nevertheless, Mackenzie King was a smart politician. He proceeded step by step. He took his time. He held the referendum in 1942, but it wasn't until 1944 that he imposed conscription. And that, alas, gave the movement time to lose steam. We saw the same thing happen recently: Robert Bourassa played for time until the movement that grew up after the collapse of Meech Lake lost steam.

People felt so hurt that there was even talk of a "racial vote": English Canada voted on one side and French Canada — today we would say the Québécois — voted on the other. The word *race*, at the time, was used to designate what's really a nation. But it truly was a vote divided in two, a "racial vote." People said yes on one side and no on the other. That's why there was incredible tension between the two communities, the two nations of Canada, and that's how the Bloc Populaire was born. Quebecers no longer had a political instrument to express their frustration. Even at the provincial level, the Godbout government was also Liberal, and a virtual puppet in the hands of the federal government. That's why people became active in the Bloc Populaire.

Gilles Gougeon: What was that?

Richard Desrosiers: It was made up of the nationalists we talked about before: people in the Action Libérale Nationale, supporters of René Chaloult,[8] people who were against the trusts. But there was also a new generation of young people who had grown up under the influence of Canon Groulx, such as André Laurendeau, who had been active in Groulx's student organizations in the thirties. There was Mayor — excuse me, the future mayor — Drapeau; there was Michel Chartrand.[9] In fact, all the people who had resisted conscription, whatever their political orientation, right or left, joined together in the Bloc Populaire.

Gilles Gougeon: And what was the Bloc Populaire's political influence?

Richard Desrosiers: It's difficult to build a party on a temporary event like that. It's difficult to maintain a party in that context, especially when you have Michel Chartrand, Jean Drapeau and André Laurendeau side by side, disciples of Canon Groulx and old Conservatives, and when your cohesion is essentially built on nationalism and the "no" to conscription. The Bloc Populaire very quickly experienced difficulties in defining its platform, because of tensions between the party leader, Laurendeau, and the financial backers such as Maxime Raymond, a wealthy man of the time. In addition, the Bloc Populaire was caught up in the election game at two levels, federal and provincial, and it was the provincial election that came first.

It's a bit strange, when you think about it, because it was a federal political context, a federal crisis. The Bloc Populaire had momentum: polls predicted it would win 20, 30, 35 per cent of the popular vote. First came the provincial election, so they ran candidates. With hindsight, it's easy to say that if they had saved their energy for the federal election a few months later, maybe the result would have been different. At the federal level there was a complete void. But at the provincial level Duplessis was still there; the Union Nationale was still there. In fact, the presence of the Bloc Populaire in the 1944 provincial election brought the Union Nationale back to power —

Gilles Gougeon: By taking away votes from the Liberals —

Richard Desrosiers: By taking away votes from the Liberals! With only 35 to 36 per cent of the vote, the Union Nationale came to power with forty-eight seats, while the provincial Liberals had almost 39 per cent of the vote. They had 4 or 5 per cent less in the popular vote, but more seats. The Bloc Populaire, with 16 per cent of the vote, won only four seats; it didn't even have the balance of power. What actually happened was that it brought about the change of government. By the way, that's happened twice in Quebec history. The RIN[10] did the same thing to Jean Lesage in 1966. You take away votes from the party in power and in the end it's the other party, which takes fewer votes but more seats, that wins.

Gilles Gougeon: So Duplessis returned to power in 1944 and stayed there until 1959. Was this the same Duplessis that we knew at the beginning? How did Duplessis's nationalism develop? Did he continue to say "No, no, no," or did he also do positive things?

Richard Desrosiers: To start with, I would say that at first Duplessis kind of exploited nationalism. It's perhaps a strong word, but I think he used nationalism for electoral purposes. He realized that Godbout, who was beaten in 1944 and again in 1948, was an easy target: he was a puppet of the federal Liberals. Characterizing Godbout in this way worked to Duplessis's political advantage. After the 1948 provincial election, which was a landslide for the Union Nationale, there were only a handful of Liberals left in the legislature, Anglophones from the West Island under an acting leader, George Marler. It was a piece of cake for Duplessis to show that the Liberals were against Quebec, that they had sold out Quebec, that they had brought in conscription. Every ill was laid at the feet of the Liberals, federal and provincial alike, while he, Duplessis, defended Quebec. There was enormous use of nationalism and autonomy for electoral purposes.

But render unto Caesar what is Caesar's — that doesn't mean that Duplessis only used nationalism and provincial autonomy for electoral purposes. He also accomplished a certain number of things, the most important of which, for the governments of the sixties, was the establishment of a provincial income tax. He managed to win this in 1954 in a power play against Louis Saint-Laurent. This was important because the Godbout provincial Liberal government had yielded all tax fields to Ottawa because of the war. When the war was over, the federal government didn't want to give it all back to the provinces, and the other Canadian provinces allowed themselves to be convinced; they allowed themselves to be bought off with subsidies. In the end, just Quebec and Ontario resisted, and finally Quebec alone. That's when Duplessis pulled off his power play, establishing a provincial income tax; he was even willing to impose double taxation. Having budgetary self-determination and the right to levy their own taxes would be extremely important for the Lesage government and all the governments that followed. This was undeniably something positive for Quebec.

There was also the fleur-de-lys flag, which today is a symbol used by all nationalist and independentist groups. You see it in Saint-Jean-Baptiste Day parades. The Quebec flag has become an important symbol of identity. In 1948, when a number of movements had been demanding a flag for a long time, Duplessis decreed by Order in Council — it took some time before he could have this measure ratified through legislation — that the fleur-de-lys would be the flag of the Quebec people. With hindsight, seeing things as we do today, we have to acknowledge that here too he made a good move. The establishment of Radio-Québec also had merit, although it was only on paper. It was important to show that it could be done because the constitution allowed it. In fact, Radio-Québec would not exist concretely until the late sixties.

Gilles Gougeon: During Duplessis's reign, did the church continue to play the same kind of role as it had played since the 1837-38 rebellions? Did the church still have the same role?

Richard Desrosiers: Yes. Until the Quiet Revolution, until the sixties, the church was an extremely important, dominant social and political force in Quebec. It still controlled the education system, so the elites still passed through its hands. The classical colleges were the favoured training grounds for our politicians. Elementary school, high school, the whole education system was in the hands of the church. The church maintained a close relationship, even a direct relationship, with governments of whatever kind. If this relationship changed, it was perhaps because of Duplessis's adroitness. Rather than the church controlling the government, Duplessis now tried to control the church. Duplessis said that the bishops ate out of his hand. Thus, he would make Mgr. Charbonneau[11] wait in the antechamber of his parliamentary office for a long time.

Gilles Gougeon: But how did Duplessis use the church in the political, social and economic spheres? What role did he have the church play?

Richard Desrosiers: Until the sixties, the church was an important social force. In city and country alike, everything was organized through the church. I made my first bank deposits in the classroom, when this or that brother had us fill out a bank deposit for a caisse populaire. It was done through the Christian Brothers or other religious communities. The church was everywhere. The Saint-Vincent-de-Paul Society, the caisse populaire, all the social assistance organizations, et cetera, were set up either in the rectory or beside it. By the way, all the caisses populaires are still located near churches. Through the parish, through its social works, the church succeeded in taking the population in hand. So it exercised total control. Like politicians before him, Duplessis knew he needed the support of the church. He relied on the same values, the same social group, to pursue his policies.

His social policies were right-wing policies, and in the area of labour relations they went very far to the right. He resorted to the provincial police and punitive legislation — legislation that would later be declared *ultra vires* or unconstitutional. Everything had to be done to break the trade union movement. On this point, even the clergy began to distance itself from Duplessis. Mgr. Charbonneau, the archbishop of Montreal, helped the Asbestos strikers by taking up a collection in the parishes in his diocese. Duplessis never forgave him for that. He asked Mgr. Roy[12] to intervene to get Charbonneau out of Montreal. The result was that Charbonneau became a chaplain in an asylum in British Columbia. Duplessis had succeeded in pushing his influence all the way to Rome to boot out — pardon the expression — Mgr. Charbonneau. And Charbonneau wasn't a nobody — he was the archbishop of Montreal.

Duplessis used the influence, the social role and the values of the clergy to his advantage. And he took them to the limit. That's why when Duplessis fell, when the Union Nationale fell, the clergy suffered the fallout. The Quiet Revolution was the beginning of a major change among our political and social elites. And the clergy would suffer for a long time for having been so closely identified with Duplessis.

I'd like to add a story. When you listen to Duplessis's speeches, he sounds like a *curé*, a parish priest, talking. When you listen to Duplessis speaking, you know this is not a Jean Lesage or a René Lévesque. Television would undoubtedly have killed Maurice Duplessis. He couldn't have made the transition. He was someone who talked like a *curé*. So in the mid-fifties, when he opened the Beauharnois dam, which was the equivalent of Manic[13] at the time, he referred to "spiritual values that are more important than material things....How fortunate that we are Catholics." It's incredible! You would think you're listening to a country *curé*, not a premier! But you realize that he was also trying to bank on tradition.

Bibliography

Black, Conrad. *Duplessis*. Toronto: McClelland and Stewart, 1977.

Boismenu, Gérard. *Le duplessisme: Politique économique et rapports de force, 1944-1960*. Montreal: Presses de l'Université de Montréal, 1981.

Comeau, Paul-André. *Le Bloc populaire, 1942-1948*. Montreal: Québec-Amérique, 1982.

Desrosiers, Richard. "Maurice Duplessis et l'autonomie provinciale." Master's thesis, University of Montreal, 1971.

Dion, Léon. *Québec 1945-2000*. Vol. 2. *Les intellectuels et le temps de Duplessis*. Quebec City: Presses de l'Université Laval, 1993.

Notes

1. Shawinigan Water and Power was the largest power-generating company in Quebec at the time and would have been a prime target of any move to nationalize electricity. It was nationalized by the Liberal government of Premier Jean Lesage in 1963. *–tr.*
2. Honoré Mercier was premier of Quebec from 1887 to 1891. *–tr.*
3. See note 1, page 65.
4. Elected in June 1960, nine months after Duplessis's death. *–tr.*
5. In 1949 members of the Canadian and Catholic Confederation of Labour went on strike against the U.S.-owned Johns-Manville Company in the town of Asbestos. Duplessis sent the provincial police into Asbestos, and the police were widely accused of abuses against the strikers. The strike helped crystallize the growing opposition to Duplessis. *–tr.*
6. The trusts were large corporations or groups of corporations that exercised undue economic power. The struggle against the trusts was a major focus of the Populist and Progressive movements in the United States in the late nineteenth and early twentieth centuries, and this focus was adopted by Quebec nationalists, who made the trusts (most of which were owned outside Quebec) a central target in the 1930s. *–tr.*
7. The provincial Liberal leader at the time. *–tr.*
8. René Chaloult was an original member of the Action Libérale Nationale and the Union Nationale, and later an opponent of Duplessis and a leader of the fight against conscription. *–tr.*
9. Later a Quebec labour leader and socialist. *–tr.*
10. The Rassemblement pour l'Indépendance Nationale, the most prominent pro-independence movement of the 1960s. *–tr.*
11. Joseph Charbonneau, archbishop of Montreal (1940-50) and opponent of Duplessis. *–tr.*
12. Maurice Roy, appointed archbishop of Quebec in 1947. *–tr.*
13. The Manicouagan dam on the North Shore of the St. Lawrence, opened in 1968, became a symbol of Quebec's industrial prowess in the 1960s. *–tr.*

Part Four

The fourth and last program covers the turbulent and dynamic period between the 1960s and the 1990s. This is the period of the Quiet Revolution; the Liberal Party of Lapalme, Lesage and Lévesque; the emergence of the state as the driving force of the economy and of national self-assertion; the establishment of independentist movements; the election of the Parti Québécois; the 1980 referendum; the repatriation of the constitution in 1982; and the failure of the Meech Lake Accord in 1990. During this period, the "French Canadians" would say that from now on they are "Québécois," and then finally, in response to the phenomenon of immigration that would change the traditional parameters of national identity, "Francophone Québécois."

The people interviewed are historians Richard Desrosiers and Robert Comeau and the political science professor Louis Balthazar.

Interview with
Richard Desrosiers (ii)

Gilles Gougeon: Mr. Desrosiers, even during the reign of Duplessis, there was still an opposition in Quebec. It couldn't have been easy to face Duplessis as leader of the opposition.

Richard Desrosiers: No. For Georges-Émile Lapalme, the fifties were very hard years. History has been unfair to Georges-Émile Lapalme, who played a very important but little-known role. To face Duplessis as leader of the opposition in the fifties wasn't easy at all. First of all, there was a denial of rights. During the fifties, the Duplessis years, there was no Hansard. It was considered a waste of money and time! So imagine what could go on in the legislature. Duplessis had complete control of the legislature, except for reporters from *Le Devoir*, like Pierre Laporte, who covered the main events. And Duplessis refused to give a press conference if there was a *Le Devoir* reporter in the room. That was how Duplessis manipulated the usual rules of parliamentary democracy.

It took extraordinary courage to be leader of the opposition in the fifties. The Union Nationale election machine had been refined to the point where the opposition would have needed a virtual landslide to win an election. In addition, in 1950 Georges-Émile Lapalme inherited a party that bore the stigma of the conscription crisis. He had to transform the party and try to give it a new political agenda. Georges-Émile Lapalme's role consisted of both keeping a little democracy in the legislature and rebuilding a Liberal Party that had an image problem. And the agenda that Georges-Émile Lapalme worked out in the late fifties was really a program for the Quiet Revolution.

Gilles Gougeon: Would you say that Georges-Émile Lapalme inspired the program of the Liberals who carried out the Quiet Revolution?

Richard Desrosiers: Inspired! He was the father of the program. Jean Lesage was chosen as leader in 1958 because they wanted a new image, and in terms of television or advertising images Georges-Émile Lapalme didn't come across so well. But the ideas for the Quiet Revolution were really Georges-Émile Lapalme's — he established the Quebec Liberal Federation, despite the opposition of the party's financial backers, and he fought to have the Liberals change their ideas about nationalism, about the state and about social policy.

Finally, when Lesage was chosen as party leader, Lapalme had enough time and perspective to write his famous essay *Pour une politique*, which was virtually a program for the Quiet Revolution and the inspiration for the Liberal election platform in 1960. But I'm not talking only about the election platform. The great ideas of the Quiet Revolution and the great reforms it put forward were all set in motion by Georges-Émile Lapalme late in his career as party leader. And in the early sixties, he was still active in the Liberal Party.

Gilles Gougeon: But when the Quebec Liberals changed leaders, they chose a man who was not well known here. Where did this Jean Lesage come from, and who was he? Was he perceived as a nationalist at the beginning?

Richard Desrosiers: No! Not at all. He had been a federal minister in the Saint-Laurent cabinet for a while. He had been in the opposition in Ottawa since the Liberals lost the election to Diefenbaker. Why did the Quebec Liberals seek out Jean Lesage? I would say that it was because he was a dedicated federalist, and they had begun to fear Georges-Émile Lapalme's ideas. You had to have cheek to set up a Quebec Liberal Federal Federation without the support of the financial backers, as he did. Inviting people to a political convention and asking them to pay to attend — no one had ever seen that in the fifties. You paid people to participate in a political convention, not the other way round!

They feared Georges-Émile Lapalme. He didn't have a good image, he was tired from his struggle against Duplessis, and Lesage seemed like a jovial, dynamic, federalist, pragmatic guy who could bring together all the opposition forces. Paul Gérin-Lajoie was also in the running to succeed Lapalme. But he was perhaps too nationalist; he was an academic and they feared he didn't have enough political skill. According to the expression that was used at the time, they wanted a *bon politicien*, a good politician, who could win elections and who had an image that didn't present any problems. That's why, in the end, Jean Lesage won the leadership. He was the choice of the federal party and the financial backers. His victory could even have caused people to worry that Georges-Émile Lapalme's efforts to change the party wouldn't bear fruit.

But fortunately, Jean Lesage was clever enough to understand that he couldn't win an election alone. To take power in Quebec, the Liberals had to organize a super-team. Fifteen years of political domination, patronage and stolen elections had to be overturned. So they needed more than a good leader — they needed a first-rate team. Lesage understood this, and the Liberals did as well. That's why they sought out Paul Gérin-Lajoie, René Lévesque, and even Georges-Émile Lapalme. The "four Ls" — the *équipe du tonnerre* (thunder squad or "hell of a team"). And that's how political change came to pass in 1960.

Gilles Gougeon: In the late fifties, did people sense that the end of the Duplessis era was coming?

Richard Desrosiers: Yes. Everywhere in Quebec there was ferment — in the trade union movement; among artists, since the *Refus global*;[1] among academics, for example the group around Father Georges-Henri Lévesque at Laval University; in journals, such as *Cité Libre*. Nationalist groups, like the Montreal Saint-Jean-Baptiste Society, were beginning to redefine nationalism by talking about the nation-state. *Le Devoir* began to reposition itself. People sensed this ferment all around them.

The best proof that it was the end of a political era was that when Paul Sauvé took power after Duplessis died, he undertook a process of change of his own. This was his *"désormais."*[2] Because he was only in office for a hundred days, we can't be sure whether he did this out of political savvy or pure opportunism, but in any case Paul Sauvé sensed that Quebec was at the end of a political era. The profound economic and social changes that had come out of the Second World War were exercising enormous pressure. The political system was cracking everywhere. In the late fifties, Quebec still had a government that represented values appropriate to the nineteenth century, a government that was even afraid of the state. In every area, things had to change. And that's what happened in 1960. The Quiet Revolution in 1960 was certainly a victory for the Lesage team and a series of political reforms that his government would undertake. But more broadly, the Quiet Revolution was also an overall change in Quebec society — in its values, elites and culture. It's very important not to associate the Quiet Revolution only with the Lesage government.

Gilles Gougeon: So, who carried out the Quiet Revolution?

Richard Desrosiers: In the political sphere, the Liberal Party, of course. Lesage, Lévesque, Gérin-Lajoie, Lapalme — each of them brought forward major reforms in his own sector. The establishment of a Department of Education was a must, as was the establishment of a Department of Cultural Affairs. There was also a proliferation of new activities in the major economic sectors, from the nationalization of electricity through the creation of the Caisse de Dépôt et Placement — which today is a wonderful instrument — to the creation of the General Investment Corporation. In the social sphere, hospital insurance and various other social measures were put forward. All these initiatives came from the government.

The political reforms secured the establishment in Quebec of the welfare state, which had been in place at the federal level since the Second World War. At the provincial level, we were a little late. This was the reason people talked about a Quiet Revolution: we had to hurry up and do in a short time what other provinces and other countries had been doing over a longer period, since the Second World War. People had to work fast, which created the impression that everything was changing. Actually, everything did change, and things got away from the Lesage government.

Lesage had nothing to do with the rise of nationalism in the sixties — on the contrary. He wasn't very happy to see that the baby he had brought into the world was growing up and getting away from him. In the area of arts and culture or the way people thought, it was the same phenomenon. In terms of religion, for example, everything collapsed; priests were defrocked and left their religious communities. The family underwent a similar development. In the mid-fifties, even if the Quebec family was not what it had once been, methods of contraception were still the traditional ones; the pill — that was no good. In 1964-65, Quebec women used birth control pills more than women in any other Western society. In ten years there was a radical change that affected ways of thinking, ideologies, culture. Everything was in motion. It was like a pot whose lid was kept in place by the Duplessis system; when someone dared to open it, it exploded, and it exploded in all directions. It probably went far beyond what Jean Lesage wanted.

Gilles Gougeon: If Jean Lesage's Liberal Party wasn't nationalist, just how do you explain the growth of nationalism that, in the end, led to René Lévesque's having to leave the party?

Richard Desrosiers: I don't believe that Jean Lesage was a nationalist, or if he was, he was a federalist first. The majority of members of the Legislative Assembly tended towards federalism, didn't believe in a renewal of nationalism and didn't want a major constitutional change. Force of circumstance led Lesage into major achievements on behalf of Quebec autonomy, but fundamentally, the leadership of his party was federalist. It didn't want to go too far, and when some measures risked offending his friends in Ottawa, Lesage drew back. For example, the establishment of a Quebec steel mill, even though that had been part of the Liberal platform for a long time. When they saw that that went against English Canadian interests, they drew back. It was Daniel Johnson, not Jean Lesage, who signed the agreements to establish Sidbec. The Liberals agreed with reforms in Quebec that were directed towards establishing the welfare state, but they drew back if there was a risk of endangering the federal link or constitutional equilibrium. Lesage was clear on that point.

But there was a militant nationalist wing in his party, grouped around René Lévesque. The nationalist wing was stronger in the cabinet than it was in the party. René Lévesque was really the leader of this wing; not that he favoured independence — let's say sovereignty. I don't think he really thought about that before 1964 or 1965. But it's clear that he was heading in that direction. You could see it in the 1962 election campaign. Look at the slogan — *"Maîtres chez nous,"* Masters in our own house. It was René Lévesque who insisted on that theme.

Lesage didn't want to nationalize electricity. At the famous special meeting of the Lesage cabinet at Lac à l'Épaule, Georges-Émile Lapalme intervened in the conflict between Lévesque, who had taken up the cause of nationalizing electricity, and Lesage, who was opposed. Lapalme was of the firm belief that if the Liberals ran on the nationalization of electricity in the next election, they would win. And to convince Lesage, he was counting on the premier's political opportunism. The Union Nationale was divided after the convention that chose Daniel Johnson as leader. The Liberals had been in power for barely two years. So Lesage took the bait and agreed to call an election on the issue of the nationalization of electricity. That was when Lévesque came up with his famous slogan *"Maîtres chez nous."* This idea went much further than even the nationalists wanted, and Lesage was trapped in this campaign. That explains why he shut Lévesque out in 1966. He told Lévesque, "You're not interfering in the election campaign; this time I'm doing it myself." And he lost.

Gilles Gougeon: How were the brakes put on this nationalist momentum that displeased the federalist elements in the Lesage government?

Richard Desrosiers: The Lesage government took a new turn around 1964-65. Economic portfolios were taken away from Kierans[3] and Lévesque and they were placed in social affairs. But inheriting the social affairs and health portfolios in 1964 meant inheriting a whole pile of problems. It was anything but a political promotion. It meant that the nationalist wing was losing influence, and the federalist wing was gaining the upper hand again.

At the same time, through a by-election, a guy named Claude Wagner was brought into the cabinet. He was a populist lawyer, a right-winger, a supporter of law and order who claimed to have fought organized crime, and he decided to show that he had had enough of nationalist demonstrations. He gave us *Samedi de la matraque* (Nightstick Saturday), when he decided to unleash the police against demonstrators who objected to Queen Elizabeth's visit to Quebec City. It was thanks to him that we got the ridiculous farce of an antiriot armoured vehicle as a weapon against nationalist demonstrations.

The government began to take a hard line against nationalists. People felt it, starting in 1964-65, when Lévesque and his friends were shut out. People felt it in the cabinet changes, in the harder line towards nationalists and in the acceptance of the Fulton-Favreau formula, where Quebec agreed to repatriation of the constitution and an amending formula. Had it not been for the campaign led by Jacques-Yvan Morin and the nationalists of the time, Quebec would have gotten into something worse than Meech Lake. People felt that Lesage was putting on the brakes. They felt the federalist wing was gaining the upper hand again.

Gilles Gougeon: So there was a split at that time.

Richard Desrosiers: There was a split between the nationalist wing and the federalist wing. But as long as he was in government, Lévesque champed at the bit — until 1966 when the Liberals suffered a painful election defeat. It was a big surprise because the polls had predicted a Liberal victory, which was actually correct, because they did take a higher percentage of the popular vote than the Union Nationale.

Gilles Gougeon: But the RIN[4] took votes away.

Richard Desrosiers: That's right.

Gilles Gougeon: So now there was a Union Nationale government that nobody had seen coming. What did the nationalists in the Liberal Party do then?

Richard Desrosiers: The nationalists in the Liberal Party no longer had the influence that came from being in charge of their departments; they no longer had the weight of the government behind them. So René Lévesque started to reflect on the constitutional question which, he said, he had ignored. It seems he consulted Georges-Émile Lapalme on this question and Lapalme told him, "Listen, to pursue the Quiet Revolution we need to go a little further on the constitutional question." Lévesque then got a group of friends together, with whom he would later put forward the manifesto describing sovereignty-association.

At first considered a wing within the Liberal Party, this minority group undertook a reappraisal of Quebec's political situation. Robert Bourassa was even indirectly associated with it. In fact, some of the Lévesque group's meetings were held in the basement of Robert Bourassa's house. But Bourassa preferred succeeding Jean Lesage as leader to getting his hands dirty. In 1967, Lévesque pressed the issue a bit further, but he knew that the battle was lost before it began. He tried to persuade the Liberal Party to undertake a constitutional review, but he didn't have a chance. And even before he could be expelled — a resolution expelling him was being prepared — René Lévesque decided to quit the party. He slammed the door and finally founded his own movement, the MSA,[5] which became the Parti Québécois.

Gilles Gougeon: When the Parti Québécois came to power a few years later, could that be called a historic moment in the development of Quebec nationalism?

Richard Desrosiers: Coming to power in 1976 marked the renewal of the Quiet Revolution and its completion. I'm not talking from a national or nationalist perspective. I say this taking into account all the reforms of the state that were carried out between 1960 and 1966, and even until 1968, because I would also put Daniel Johnson in the line of political leaders of the Quiet Revolution. Jean-Jacques Bertrand in 1968 and Bourassa in 1970 put on the brakes. Except for the Castonguay reform,[6] the Quiet Revolution was really over by the beginning of the 1970s.

In 1976, however, it was taken up again. There was a renewal of the Quiet Revolution, as seen in the slogans, the reforms that were pursued and the role of the state. This included giving the Caisse de Dépôt et Placement, for example, a role as an agent of economic intervention to support Quebec businessmen, which Bourassa had refused to do. In 1976, it's clear that we were living in a historic moment because the Quiet Revolution was taken up again, including its nationalist dimension. But it wasn't a triumph for the independence movement or the sovereignist movement; I don't think anyone saw it that way. It was more a question of taking up again what had been started in the sixties, and it didn't so much represent a victory for nationalist forces as accession to sovereignty or an associated form of sovereignty would have signified. The proof was the result of the referendum. I don't think the Quebec people, or even the Parti Québécois, were perhaps as ready as all that.

Gilles Gougeon: Let's get to 1980, to the referendum. It posed a question that was a bit convoluted, that wasn't very strong, but that gave Quebecers an opportunity to take a stand on this proposal. In the overall development of French Canadian and Quebec nationalism, how should we see this stage and the result of the 1980 referendum?

Richard Desrosiers: The result of the 1980 referendum signified the beginning of the great discouragement. For nationalists, for intellectuals, it was a terrible morning after, when hopes that they had entertained for ten, twelve, twenty years were dashed. But at the same time — and we see this with hindsight — what the Yes side was missing, what the sovereignist movement was missing, was the support of Quebec businessmen. In forming a good government, Lévesque was aiming to show that working to build the Quebec state would ultimately benefit everybody, including businessmen. But the evidence wasn't completely in place in 1980.

To be sure, the various forms of government intervention in the economy had shown businessmen that Quebec had some powerful tools — Hydro-Quebec and the Caisse de Dépôt et Placement both demonstrated it. But they still had the impression that in business they needed the federal big brother. Even if St. James Street was renamed Rue Saint-Jacques, people in the Quebec business community still had the impression that they needed Ottawa or they needed Ontario. But in fact — and even Bourassa contributed to this — the 1980s demonstrated to businessmen that this was not true.

The debate on free trade with the United States showed this clearly. Quebec businessmen, Montreal businessmen, could succeed. They didn't need the federal big brother. This was a new element in the constitutional debate and in the current rise of nationalism. This time, the results of a referendum would have a chance of being positive because additional social strata would support Quebec's becoming sovereign. It wasn't just youth, the intellectuals, the petty bourgeoisie. It was the businessmen, too! The Rue Saint-Jacques had become more nationalist and militant than some of our universities, and that proved that there had been a change.

So in the short term, 1980 brought about a great discouragement. But it wasn't death; everything didn't end. The rebirth of the movement on different foundations proves that. The constitutional question was not settled in 1980. It's still not settled. At certain times, it will be a factor that will stir people up. I think that the Parti Québécois under Pierre-Marc Johnson was wrong in thinking that it had to abandon the sovereignty plank. In thinking that the whole thing had lasted only a decade or so, they misunderstood the history of Quebec nationalism. They didn't see that the roots of the movement went back to the eighteenth and nineteenth centuries. They didn't understand that if there is a constant in the history of the Quebec people, it is the rise in national self-assertion and the questioning of the link with the Canadian whole. That wasn't just going to grind to a halt with the 1980 referendum.

Bibliography

Comeau, Robert et al., eds. *Jean Lesage et l'éveil d'une nation: Les débuts de la révolution tranquille.* Quebec City: Presses de l'Université Laval, 1989.

Godin, Pierre. *La Révolution tranquille.* Vol. 1. *La fin de la grande noirceur.* Montreal: Boréal, 1991.

———. *La Révolution tranquille.* Vol. 2. *La difficile recherche de l'égalité.* Montreal: Boréal, 1991.

———. *Les frères divorcés.* Montreal: Éditions de l'Homme, 1986.

Lévesque, René. *An Option for Quebec.* Toronto: McClelland and Stewart, 1968.

Marsolais, Claude V. *Le référendum confisqué: Histoire du référendum québécois du 20 mai 1980.* Montreal: VLB Éditeur, 1992.

Notes

1. Manifesto published by a group of artists led by Paul-Émile Borduas in 1948. –*tr.*
2. "From now on." Duplessis died in September 1959 and was succeeded by Sauvé. Immediately there was a sense of impending change, symbolized by the word *désormais* used by the new premier to indicate that henceforth things would be different. Sauvé himself died in January 1960. Five months later, his successor Antonio Barrette narrowly lost a provincial election to Jean Lesage's Liberals. –*tr.*
3. Eric Kierans came into the Lesage cabinet as minister of revenue in 1963 and was another of the strong ministers in the government. –*tr.*
4. See note 10, page 83.
5. Mouvement Souveraineté-Association, or sovereignty-association movement. –*tr.*
6. Reform of social services carried out by Claude Castonguay, minister of social affairs in the Bourassa government from 1970 to 1973. –*tr.*

Interview with
Robert Comeau (ii)

Gilles Gougeon: Mr. Comeau, in the 1950s, a man made his way onto the political scene and, even though you hear his name a lot, not much is known about him today. I'm speaking of Georges-Émile Lapalme. Tell me a little about Georges-Émile Lapalme.

Robert Comeau: Georges-Émile Lapalme was a person who played a very important role. He was leader of the Quebec Liberal Party from 1950 to 1958. Mr. Lapalme was treated with contempt by Duplessis and he had only a few seats in the Legislative Assembly, but he brought about a fundamental change in the orientation of the Quebec Liberal Party. A friend of the arts, highly literate, with a political career in opposition that had been riddled with failures, he guided the Liberal Party in taking a major turn on both social and national issues. In 1958, when he was preparing the party's election platform, he wrote what was really a manifesto in which he presented all the reforms that he considered essential for the development of Quebec. The Quiet Revolution was Lapalme's idea, and Jean Lesage took his inspiration from Lapalme.

In 1958, he realized that the Quebec Liberal Party had made a mistake when it hadn't supported Duplessis's demand for recovery of the personal income tax from Ottawa. At the time, Lapalme had supported Louis Saint-Laurent. But Duplessis had won and that victory in 1954 was extremely important: it provided the Quebec government with resources. In the document that he drew up in 1958, *Pour une politique*, Lapalme showed that he was a true visionary. He spoke of a new role for the Quebec state, which he wanted to see advance the economic liberation of Quebec. He wanted to use the Quebec state as an instrument of economic liberation. After a term as a member of Parliament in Ottawa, Lapalme changed his attitude towards the Quebec question. He became very nationalist. In the late fifties, he proposed concrete reform measures that would be submitted to the Quebec electorate. Instead of counting on Ottawa to fight Duplessis's policies, he put forward a progressive nationalism. This proposal won the support of many democrats who were disillusioned with the Union Nationale's policies.

His ideas would be taken up by Lesage and, even more important, by the senior civil servants who surrounded René Lévesque — André Marier, Claude Morin, Jacques Parizeau, Roland Parenteau, et cetera. They sought to have the Quebec state play a much more significant role. Quebec nationalism was becoming linked with social reform and no longer had anything to do with Duplessis's nationalism, which was linked with a conservative ideology. It was Lapalme, in my opinion, who brought about this turn, this change in the Quebec Liberal Party's orientation.

Gilles Gougeon: Would you go so far as to say that Georges-Émile Lapalme was one of the fathers of the Quiet Revolution?

Robert Comeau: Oh yes! Certainly. I think we need to rehabilitate Georges-Émile Lapalme, who is not very well known. Even now I don't think he is given the credit he deserves, and yet he was the Liberal Party's thinker at the time, much more so than Jean Lesage. Lesage was in charge of putting these policies into effect, but it was Lapalme who worked out the political program and formulated it clearly. This program *Pour une politique*, which Lapalme wrote in 1958, was published recently. It was much more than an election platform; it really contained the major directives that would be followed for the next twenty years. The whole period from 1960 to 1980 was influenced by Georges-Émile Lapalme. In the end, his program was the program of the Quiet Revolution. And it was this program that attracted René Lévesque to the Liberal Party. The major reforms proposed in it completely seduced him. The program put forward a vision of a modern, progressive Quebec and included a new and much more progressive definition of nationalism.

Gilles Gougeon: Do you think that René Lévesque, the René Lévesque of the Mouvement Souveraineté-Association, of the Parti Québécois, was also influenced by Lapalme?

Robert Comeau: I'm convinced of it. It was Lapalme who supported such measures as the nationalization of electricity. At the time, he persuaded Jean Lesage to adopt this measure. In a short memo dated 1966, after the Liberal Party's defeat, it was again Lapalme who exhorted Lévesque to continue to define his constitutional position, while lamenting the Liberals' lack of a constitutional position in 1966. René Lévesque didn't hesitate to consult him in 1966. Remember that Lapalme had resigned as minister of cultural affairs in 1964 on the grounds that Jean Lesage's party undervalued the department that he had created and had fought for in an effort to increase its resources. But in 1966, it was still Lapalme who was advising René Lévesque and encouraging him to pursue his work in founding the MSA. I don't think Lapalme's role as an adviser to Lévesque is talked about much, but it seems very important to me. Lapalme's role in the great change of the sixties has been underestimated.

Gilles Gougeon: You pointed out that resisting Duplessis in the forties and early fifties meant resisting a form of conservatism, and at the same time it meant resisting a form of nationalism, which was Duplessis's nationalism. Wasn't that what people like Trudeau, Pelletier and Marchand were doing when they resisted Duplessis? They were resisting his conservatism, but at the same time they were resisting his nationalism.

Robert Comeau: Indeed. Progress seemed to come from Ottawa. In these years, Ottawa put forward social policies, while Quebec had more of a policy of non-intervention. Social policies were rejected. It wasn't until the late fifties that people said "Couldn't there be a way, in Quebec itself, of being nationalist and progressive at the same time? Couldn't the Quebec government adopt social measures?" This came after the Tremblay Report,[1] in 1956, when Quebec nationalist intellectuals said for the first time: "We have to change our attitude towards the state. It's possible to have progressive policies in Quebec City itself."

In other words, let's stop saying no to Ottawa, let's stop demanding autonomy in a purely negative way. Let's put things more positively by saying that social measures should be adopted and that it should happen in Quebec City. And that's how the whole constitutional problem got opened up, because the Quebec government didn't have adequate powers or the financial resources to do that. This was the beginning of the fight to recover powers and taxes, and it took place around 1956-57. Lapalme came onside at almost the same time as the Tremblay Commission, which recommended that the Quebec government adopt an interventionist policy, that it shouldn't leave the initiative to Ottawa, as had been the case up until then.

In 1942, with the Marsh Report,[2] Ottawa had adopted an interventionist policy for Canada. This policy was applied along with federal centralization to strengthen Canadian unity. In Quebec, it was twenty years later that a desire for government intervention showed up, and it was because people like Lapalme wanted to have the Quebec state play a much more important role. This is where the beginning of the Quiet Revolution should be situated. People's attitude towards the state changed. They stopped seeing the state as an adversary or a socialist threat. They said that in Quebec, where Francophones are a majority, the state could play an important role in the economic development of the collectivity.

Gilles Gougeon: But in your opinion, why did people like Trudeau, Marchand and Pelletier not support Quebec nationalism?

Robert Comeau: They were against the conservatism associated with Duplessis's nationalism and at the same time against all Quebec nationalism, because according to them it was the reason Quebec was politically and economically behind. Trudeau was fiercely opposed to the French Canadian Catholic nationalist elites. He struck an internationalist pose in *Cité Libre*, but it has become clear that he was above all a Canadian nationalist. In his opinion, only Canadian nationalism could bring progress.

He recognized two official languages, but he never recognized the existence of a Québécois nation in Quebec. Trudeau never wanted to acknowledge the existence of two nations; he rejected the ideas of André Laurendeau and the analyses of the Laurendeau-Dunton Commission,[3] which pointed out the need to recognize not only two official languages but also two distinct societies with two official cultures. Trudeau replaced biculturalism with multiculturalism. Laurendeau died in 1968. In 1971 Trudeau, as prime minister, brought in legislation on multiculturalism: it was a way of denying the existence of the Québécois nation.

Gilles Gougeon: Since you mentioned André Laurendeau, I'd like to go back to the thirties when Laurendeau was the leader of a nationalist youth movement. How did the youth and their movements fit in relative to other nationalist organizations?

Robert Comeau: Besides the main tendency, which favoured autonomy, there was another tendency, a marginal one, I would say, which was strongest among youth — among youth movements. This was a frankly separatist tendency, which lasted only two years. There were the Jeunesses Patriotes, the Jeunes Laurentiens and a number of journals: I'm thinking of *Vivre*, among others.

The newspaper *La Nation*, with Paul Bouchard as its editor, was clearly the most important of these publications, the one that lasted the longest. At the very beginning, this newspaper said it favoured outright separation. Of course, the people at *La Nation* said they were disciples of Groulx, but Groulx had never taken the leap to official support for independence. Nevertheless, he encouraged them in their separatist tendency. He was their intellectual mentor.

These young people were fierce anti-communists and they quite openly took their inspiration from the far right in Italy, Portugal and Spain. So they were imbued with corporatist and anti-communist ideas. They prided themselves on being more anti-communist than anyone else in Quebec. But at the same time, they were separatists. This didn't last long, about two years, because when the war began they came around to a more moderate position, and a more Canadian nationalist position in relation to Britain. Paul Bouchard, who had been the editor of *La Nation*, would become the chief organizer of the Union Nationale, and he would remain in that position until 1959. So this tendency ended up converging with Duplessis's conservative nationalist positions. And it was only around 1959 that a new separatist tendency appeared again, with the Alliance Laurentienne and the journal *La Laurentie*. Raymond Barbeau took up the ideas that Paul Bouchard had expressed between 1936 and 1938. So there was a kind of continuity in the right-wing separatist current. On the other hand, the RIN[4] was not directly part of this current. It was more of a centrist party that began in the sixties and wanted to be seen as distinct from the Alliance Laurentienne.

What I find striking is the way the independence movement has sometimes been associated with the far right, as in the thirties, while in the sixties the separatist movement was associated more with the left. In the sixties there was talk of decolonization, and even a revolutionary tendency that linked independence with socialism, as you can see by looking through the journal *Parti Pris* (1963-68). The independentist tendency has actually been associated with two diametrically opposed socio-economic programs. And I would maintain that the PQ now has more of a centrist program. When you look at history, independentist ideology has been associated with different social tendencies and different economic programs.

Gilles Gougeon: There has been a kind of pluralism within nationalism —

Robert Comeau: That's right. As history has unfolded, there has not been just one tendency. And nationalism has taken on a variety of expressions at the same time.

Gilles Gougeon: Now I'd like to talk about a man who I'm sure is unknown to the general public: Maurice Séguin. In what way has this great history teacher been important to understanding and exploring the nationalist movement and the Quebec identity?

Robert Comeau: I think that Maurice Séguin was the most controversial, the most misunderstood, and yet the most important historian of modern Quebec. I think that through his students, Maurice Séguin has been more influential than you can imagine. He taught several generations starting in 1948. He held Canon Groulx's[5] chair in the history department at the University of Montreal from 1948 on, and he died in 1984. Throughout those years, he really devoted himself to teaching. As a teacher he didn't publish much, but he taught a very large number of students and trained the first generations of modern Quebec independentists. He taught Pierre Bourgault, Noël Vallerand, Denis Vaugeois, Jean-Marc Léger; he also educated many teachers and intellectuals in his conception of the history of the two Canadas.

He was original in that he broke with Canon Groulx. He had a much more "political" conception of nationalism than Canon Groulx, for whom nationalism was more cultural. For Groulx, nationalism was more a defence of culture, religion, traditions, heritage, et cetera. For Séguin, nationalism encompassed a lot more. It meant essentially to seek, to express — and also to defend, but primarily to seek and to express — mastery of a people's political, economic and cultural life. So it was much more inclusive.

And for us, it also corresponded to the period of decolonization. Maurice Séguin seemed much closer to theories of decolonization than to the theories of Canon Groulx. He was getting ready for the separatist struggle and he went back to the essential point, which for him was the defeat of the Quebec people in 1760. He was obsessed by the problem of his nation. The way he experienced the tragedy of Quebec was absolute and excessive. He spoke passionately to us about what he saw as the main problem: that the Quebec people had been put in a minority position in a federal system. That, for him, was the essential form that oppression took. In a federal system, Quebec was a minority, and increasingly so. This was quite apart from what he considered secondary forms of oppression. If French Canadians were mistreated or if the use of French was banned, as in 1840, those questions were secondary ones. The main question was structural: the fact was that, because it was put in a minority position, this society could not be in charge of its own political life.

What was striking in his thought was the emphasis he placed on the interdependence among political, economic and cultural factors. A people couldn't be culturally sovereign if it didn't have mastery of its political life. So he always drew out the links among economic, political and cultural factors and spoke of a people's need not to be "displaced." He saw oppression as displacement. He believed that for individuals and peoples alike, acting on one's own, being autonomous, was a source of enrichment and experience.

In the federal system, representatives of the other society were the majority. A majority of those representatives were dominant; they made the decisions. In this context, the minority society was necessarily appropriated. According to him, the Quebec nation was not just a society. Much more precisely, it was an oppressed, appropriated people in the context of a federal system. Maurice Séguin analysed this situation in depth — what he called a "sociology of the national question" — and he believed that theory was very important. In this sense, Maurice Séguin can be considered the theoretician of the contemporary independence movement. He worked on his theories for years before publishing them; it took him fifteen years to write his famous work on the sociology of the national question.

This work is very dense, but it enables us to reinterpret the history of the two Canadas. He proposed a new interpretive framework that would make possible a new reading of the known facts. Because what interested him most was the high political history of Quebec, he rehabilitated a kind of political history. At the same time, he established his distance from Groulx. Where Groulx had celebrated New France, Séguin was much more severe. He somewhat cynically pointed out the consequences of the defeat in 1760 for the conquered people. And he demonstrated these consequences in every area: political, cultural, economic. Séguin was anything but a reassuring historian. His was a tragic vision of the destiny of the Quebec nation, deprived of its indispensable independence. His was what people have called "dark history."

Gilles Gougeon: Do you agree with those who say that Maurice Séguin brought us from a French Canadian identity to a Quebec identity?

Robert Comeau: Yes, indeed — that was one of the characteristics of his nationalism. His nationalism was more closely linked to the territory and the state of Quebec. He was no longer attached to the Francophones of Canada as a whole, as an ethnic group or culture. He introduced us to territorial nationalism: he wanted to create a country with a national state in Quebec. It was no longer a question of begging for an unattainable equality in a federal system where French Canadians would always be a minority.

Séguin emphasized the absolute indispensability of independence for a normal people. He showed how this question of independence is essential for a people. However, he had doubts about whether it was possible for the Quebec people to achieve independence. So on the one hand, he saw the tragedy of this conquered nation, in a minority position, for which independence was a desirable end. But on the other hand, he said "It is so well kept, maybe the best kept nation in the world, and these golden chains make its liberation difficult to achieve." So because Quebec was well kept by others in the current federal system, he doubted that it could achieve independence.

It is in this sense that the school of nationalists at the University of Montreal has been called the "dark school." When we were students, at that time, we tried to persuade Séguin that if independence was desirable, then everything had to be done to make it possible. Clearly, Séguin always tried to see the situation objectively, never underestimating the adversary. He was very critical of federalists, but he was also critical of what he called "optimistic independentists," showing that the forces of the status quo should not be underestimated. The reasons why other groups wanted federalism and Canadian unity should not be underestimated.

In other words, he could see the point of view of the adversary and study it very objectively, showing what the interests of various groups were, the interests of the conquerors as well as those of the conquered. It was important to him to understand the arguments of those who were in favour of federalism. He knew the Durham Report well. Durham had a realistic vision of the future of British North America. But essentially, Séguin's course was an unrelenting critique of the federal system for a minority people. He drew both from the present and from history, for example the history of Louisiana, to make the national question understood. And it was enlightening for those of us who were his students. He was one of the intellectuals who led the effort to redefine nationalism, to define what has been called "neo-nationalism." I don't like the expression *neo-nationalism*, but that is the expression that was used to designate this new and much more pertinent definition of nationalism. Séguin said that all nationalism is necessarily separatist. He didn't win unanimous approval among historians when he said things like that. So he was a very controversial historian, not well known, because he did very little public speaking. He gave a few lectures on television in 1962, but he made few public appearances. He was a professor who devoted himself to his students, who published little, but who in my opinion was enormously influential. Among Quebec historians, he was undoubtedly the most important, although he hasn't received the recognition he deserves.

Bibliography

Comeau, Robert, ed. *Maurice Séguin, historien du pays québécois, vu par ses contemporains, suivi de "Les Normes."* Montreal: VLB Éditeur, 1987.

Comeau, Robert, and Beaudry, Lucille, eds. *André Laurendeau, un intellectuel d'ici.* Quebec City: Presses de l'Université Laval, 1990.

Lapalme, Georges-Émile. *Pour une politique: Le programme de la révolution tranquille.* Montreal: VLB Éditeur, 1988.

Léonard, Jean-François. *Georges-Émile Lapalme.* Quebec City: Presses de l'Université Laval, 1988.

Notes

1. Report of the Quebec Royal Commission of Inquiry on Constitutional Problems. *–tr.*
2. Leonard Marsh, *Report on Social Security for Canada. –tr.*

3. The Royal Commission on Bilingualism and Biculturalism, which was formed in 1963 and issued the first two volumes of its report in 1967. *–tr.*

4. See note 10, page 83. *–tr.*

5. See note 1, p. 65. *–tr.*

Interview with Louis Balthazar

Gilles Gougeon: Mr. Balthazar, before talking to you, we heard from historians who spoke to us about the past, starting with the beginning, with New France. But with you, we are engaging in a more delicate and dangerous exercise, because we are discussing the contemporary period. How would you describe contemporary nationalism in Quebec?

Louis Balthazar: First of all, I have to say that it is a profoundly different kind of nationalism from the one that existed until roughly the Second World War. It's so different, this contemporary nationalism, that we've given it a different name: it's no longer called French Canadian nationalism but rather Quebec nationalism. It's so different that many people believed they first had to repudiate the old nationalism before adopting the new one. During the 1950s, large portions of the Quebec elites declared that they were anti-nationalist, because to be nationalist meant tradition, it meant being closed in on ourselves, it meant closing the windows to the outside world. It assumed a fairly suffocating, homogeneous, ethnic conception of the French Canadian nation: the old concept of *pure-laine*[1] French Canadians, closely tied to the Catholic religion.

With the Quiet Revolution, as you know, all of that was called into question and suddenly what had been traditional nationalism took on a decidedly modern appearance. The nationalism of the sixties was a nationalism that very soon came to see itself as secular, and hence detached and independent from the Catholic religion practised by most French Canadians. It also came to see itself as outward looking, a point that may not have been sufficiently emphasized. Often, when you say the word *nationalism*, it makes you think of people who are closed in on themselves, who aren't interested in what's going on outside their country — who build walls around their nation, as it were. But that is not what Quebec nationalism is, neither for most Quebecers nor for their leaders. On the contrary, Quebec nationalists are often people who have travelled widely, people who realized, for example, that Canadian missions abroad didn't always represent us well and there were people who didn't speak French in Canadian consulates and embassies. These were people who, travel-

ling in the world, needed to have a clearer and more precise identity
— the Quebec identity.

So overall, it is wrong to say that Quebec nationalists are people
who are closed in on themselves. On the contrary, Quebec nationalism is very compatible with openness to the world and the practice
of international relations. The Quebec government started opening
missions in foreign countries. This nationalism has to do with speaking about Quebec to others — or at least as much with that as with
speaking about Quebec to ourselves.

Another new characteristic of nationalism, a very important one
in my opinion, may not have been evident right away. As soon as
the nation was defined in a Quebec perspective, that is in a territorial
perspective, we were asserting that what we belonged to was Francophone Quebec. In other words, if we were going to build a Francophone society, we would build it in Quebec where we had a critical
mass and we could do this.

In addition, as soon as we think about Quebec, we inevitably think
in terms of a multi-ethnic dimension, because Quebec is not a purely
Francophone or purely French Canadian entity. There are immigrants
in Quebec — immigrants whom we are asking to adopt the French
language, by the way. There are Anglophones in Quebec. If we
suddenly define ourselves as Québécois, it becomes contradictory to
define ourselves according to a purely ethnic dimension. We no
longer have the right to do that. *Québécois pure laine, Québécois de
vieille souche*[2] — to my mind these are expressions that no longer
make sense, because Quebec inevitably has to become even more
multi-ethnic than it is now. I know that in practice there are a lot of
Quebec nationalists who don't think this way, who — alas! —
sometimes even have attitudes that are racist or bordering on racism
and who tend to define a Québécois as if it means a French Canadian
exclusively.

But if you look at the dynamic of Quebec nationalism, it has to
become, and is inevitably already becoming, a multi-ethnic reality,
a concept that encompasses people who are of diverse origins. This
is very important, because people from outside often regard Quebec
nationalism as an ethnic movement, a movement to advance a particular ethnic group. In Canada as a whole, this has been a major
source of confusion, because members of various Canadian ethnic
groups tend to believe that French Canadians are unjustly privileged
in relation to the other ethnic groups that make up Canada. Well, the

idea of Quebec is not and cannot be an ethnic idea; it has to be a cultural idea, encompassing people of diverse origins.

Gilles Gougeon: What is it that you speak of when you speak of contemporary nationalism in Quebec?

Louis Balthazar: It is very important to define the word *nationalism*, because in the French literature on the subject, for example, nationalism is often defined as being the equivalent of chauvinism, the equivalent of extreme fanaticism: an ideology that engenders hatred of others. It is very clear that the way the word is used in Quebec does not correspond to this view. We have all met people who call themselves nationalists and who clearly don't correspond to this definition. I'm not saying that there are no fanatics in Quebec, but not all Quebec nationalists are fanatics or people who cultivate hatred of our neighbours or other people. On the contrary, many people call themselves nationalists and find that English-speaking Canadians are very appealing and that Americans are also very appealing.

I think it would be helpful to define nationalism in a neutral manner. I can say: "I belong to a people, to a nation. It's not the most important thing in the world but it does assume a degree of importance for me, so that I can show my national affiliation when I travel abroad, for example. I live in society and I believe that some things work better when they are done among people of the same culture, belonging to the same nation and living by the same customs." But with the same breath, I can say I like lots of other peoples. I can even imagine living elsewhere, leaving my nation. I don't make it a kind of absolute. It is possible to value the nation to the point of placing it higher than all other values and linking everything to the nation — then it becomes fanatical nationalism. But it is also possible, it seems to me, to cultivate a moderate form of nationalism to the extent that the nation does not become an absolute priority.

Gilles Gougeon: So you find that the current expression of nationalism is more open than it was in the past?

Louis Balthazar: I think so. Although again today, nationalism shows up in all kinds of ways. Some I would consider excessive and others, acceptable. Other judgements could also be made. But it's a bad thing to give such a pejorative meaning to the word from the outset so that any form of nationalism is condemned in advance.

Gilles Gougeon: In the eighties, we had what was called economic nationalism. Do you see the measures that the government took to make it possible for small businesses in Quebec to get started and prosper as a manifestation of nationalism?

Louis Balthazar: They certainly are, and they're also an effect of what happened in the sixties. It's a delayed effect, if you like. What happened in the sixties? The Caisse de Dépôt et Placement was established in 1966. In 1963 there was the nationalization of electricity. At the same time, the Quebec government created a number of economic instruments to give more control of the economy to Quebecers. The effects of this development were slow in making themselves felt. They were felt first at the level of government, in terms of government intervention. With time these instruments, the instruments of the Quiet Revolution, finally produced an entrepreneurship rooted in Quebec, private enterprise rooted in Quebec; better, if you like, an authentically Francophone Québécois economic network.

This didn't exist in the sixties. The Quebec economic network was an Anglophone network. As a result, many young Quebecers felt a bit inhibited there, even if they spoke English. Today there is an economic community, a business community, in which people speak French among themselves, although of course they communicate with the rest of the world in English — there's no doubt about that. I think that's a direct product of what happened during the Quiet Revolution. It has often been said that this was a contradiction, as if the Quiet Revolution was a socialist adventure. That's not true. The Quiet Revolution was made by people whose philosophy was liberal. It was primarily a bourgeois revolution, and its most obvious fruit — its ripest fruit, I might say — was the economic nationalism of the eighties.

Gilles Gougeon: In your view, have other instruments, other agencies, had an impact on the development of Quebec's national identity?

Louis Balthazar: Yes, and it's a funny thing, I'll tell you: an agency that in my opinion has contributed a lot, perhaps the most, is a federal agency. Television came to Canada in 1952. CBC television was established and, since there were Francophones and Anglophones in Canada, two networks had to be set up right away. The primary objective of the CBC has always been to bring Canadians closer to one another. The CBC French network, by force of circumstance, was in Quebec simply because the critical mass of Francophones was there, and what did it do? It brought Quebecers closer to one another, especially during the fifties. It transmitted a kind of image of ourselves as Quebecers, and it transmitted this image to people in all regions of Quebec. Think of the popularity of someone like René Lévesque, as well as other journalists such as André Laurendeau — it was the medium of the CBC French network that made them known and that allowed Quebecers to talk to one another.

Later, the French network was extended to all of Canada. But even today, inevitably — I don't think there's any ill will involved — given that a substantial majority of Francophones live in Quebec, the CBC French network still transmits a Quebec image. Whatever its leaders think, and whatever politicians say, I think there's nationalism in the CBC French network. It's a moderate nationalism, expressed without fanaticism, but in my opinion its existence is inevitable. The CBC French network is the Francophone instrument par excellence in Canada, and even if there are minorities everywhere across Canada, the Canadian Francophone community is organized and institutionalized primarily in Quebec. That, by the way, was the essence of the Quiet Revolution.

The Quiet Revolution was, first of all, the realization that if we are to build a modern society — that is an institutional network or a communications network that will make it possible for us to live in a modern way, to express ourselves and catch up with what's happening elsewhere in the world — the place where we Francophones can do it in a fully developed way with a chance of success is in Quebec. So the Quiet Revolution, inevitably, established a network within Quebec. That's what Quebec is. It's expressed in all sorts of ways: Quebec autonomy, special status, sovereignty, sovereignty-association or the national state of French Canadians. What all these expressions come down to is that for us Francophones in North America, Quebec is the place par excellence for our modern existence, our communications, our social life.

And I think the great majority of us have no intention of sacrificing this. That's what the constitutional issue has been for the last thirty years. Mr. Trudeau invited us to sacrifice it, offering us Canadian bilingualism in exchange. For us, the Quebec identity — a Quebec identity that has its own means of expressing itself, even if it has to be pursued within Canada — is a more precious thing than making Canada as a whole bilingual.

Gilles Gougeon: When you describe all the political and the socio-political expressions of nationalism, as you have just done, I have the impression that it inevitably involves the nationalism of a majority. It involves a consensus around this conception. What is your assessment of the current situation? Is this consensus stalled or is it developing?

Louis Balthazar: I think a majority of Quebecers have always believed in the Quebec identity. That's why in the referendum, the No side was very careful to use a very shrewd slogan so that it would win; they said, *"Mon non est québécois"* — My no is Québécois. That meant "You can vote No, but you will still be a Québécois, you won't lose your Quebec identity." Well, in my view and in the view of many other people, the 1982 constitution, as it was conceived, didn't leave any more room for the Quebec identity. Very simply, I believe, that is why a majority of Quebecers rejected it. To come back to the question of a consensus, I'm very interested in that because I think that nationalism here will never lead to anything unless we express a strong consensus. Otherwise, we will never be victorious and we will never succeed in constituting this Quebec reality. We have to search out that consensus and I think we can find it.

I think we could get a consensus of 75 per cent of the people in Quebec — people who believe in Quebec, who believe in the Quebec identity, who are committed to expressing it and prepared to put it into effect up to a point. And if, in the future, we have a referendum, if we were to take some action, a forward step towards a form of sovereignty or a constitutional status that suits us, I don't think we would get anywhere unless we had the support of that 75 per cent. That is, we have to take steps to make the referendum bipartisan. Whatever question people are asked, whether it's about sovereignty, sovereignty-association or Quebec's presence in a supranational entity, Liberals and Péquistes would have to campaign side by side for the Yes. Then I think we would have a powerful instrument in our hands. It's the only instrument we have — the democratic expression of a large majority. I'm not saying we absolutely have to establish a rule from the start that the Yes would not be valid unless it got 60 or 65 per cent of the vote. But in practice, if a referendum ends up producing a 75 per cent Yes vote, then we have a tool, then we have a weapon in our hands, then we've really won something.

Gilles Gougeon: Since you've studied the development of nationalism, what is your feeling, or what is your observation, about the oft-expressed idea that nationalism is dead? We have seen nationalism die a number of deaths. Have you ever had the impression that nationalism could have been dead at any time, or is it like a bulb that pushes up shoots at regular intervals?

Louis Balthazar: I did have this impression when I was very young, because in the late forties, if anyone in my circle used the word *nationalism*, it referred to a completely outdated, old-fashioned reality for which we had the utmost contempt. I sincerely believed at that time that my grandfather's nationalism was finished. But I saw nationalism reappear in the sixties with new vigour and, as I said, with a new definition. So now when someone says to me, "Nationalism is finished," I don't believe it any more, because having studied it, I see nationalism as a phenomenon that has the ability to rise again just when people think it's finished. And if you look at our history, you could have thought it was finished in 1840 with the Durham Report, after the Patriotes were crushed. Well, it came back afterwards. You could have thought it was finished in the 1950s. You could have thought it was finished in 1976 when Trudeau said "Nationalism is dead in Quebec." You could have thought it was finished after the October Crisis. People thought it was finished in 1980.

And it always comes back. The simple fact that we are a minority in North America will always lead us to remind the majority — which will invariably tend to forget us when it's not treating us with contempt — that we exist, that we have rights, and that we intend to affirm our collective existence. Now, there might come a day when Quebecers will be completely assimilated. On that day, there will no longer be any Quebec nationalism. Quebec nationalism doesn't have a promise of eternal life, but as long as there are Francophones in sufficient numbers in North America, it will always show up.

If you look elsewhere in the world, you find similar phenomena. Think of all the national feelings, all the feelings of belonging that are reappearing in the former Soviet Union with a vigour no one would have suspected after seventy years of being steamrolled by Marxism. The same thing is happening in central Europe, in what used to be the Austrian Empire, where national affiliations are now taking on considerable importance. I think it's a phenomenon that dies hard and that tends to show up periodically.

Gilles Gougeon: Essentially, the whole debate concerns the lines along which people identify themselves. Should it be as Canadians or as Québécois? For example, since 1867, there have been at least three prime ministers who were French Canadians, who were Francophones.[3] Didn't that ever encourage French Canadians, or more recently Québécois, to consider themselves a bit more Canadian rather than Québécois?

Louis Balthazar: Each time Canada has been governed by a Francophone prime minister, there has been a wave of euphoria among Canadian nationalists, let's say, and among English-speaking Canadians — among people who believe in Canada and in Canadian unity. And each time, people believed that since French Canadians could take pride in having one of their own at the top, they would become unhyphenated Canadians and would no longer identify themselves as French Canadians. And, in fact, it worked a bit each time. Laurier, Saint-Laurent and Trudeau all had a lot of support and were very popular in French Canada, in Quebec. But after each one's reign, there was always a wave of nationalism. In 1911, when Laurier lost power, he lost in part because of the nationalists led by Bourassa. What was the Quiet Revolution if not a response to Saint-Laurent's pan-Canadianism, a specifically Quebec reaction to this movement? And what's happening right now, in my view, is in large part a response to Pierre Elliott Trudeau's proposal of Canadian unity. So you see, each time they tried to go too far, a tendency to affirm Quebec or French Canada showed up.

Essentially, there's nothing diabolical in what Quebecers want, what French Canadians want. I think Quebecers love Canada and are prepared to live in a country called Canada. They've shown it on a number of occasions. But their immediate sense of belonging, their primary patriotism, is directed towards Quebec. To the extent that Quebecers can be Quebecers first and then Canadian, I believe their Canadianism can go quite a long way. But what's happening now, or at least what we hear from many English-speaking Canadians, is the invitation "Be Canadians first and then Quebecers." And I don't think you're about to get Quebecers to accept that.

Bibliography

Balthazar, Louis. *Bilan du nationalisme au Québec: Politique et société*. Montreal: L'Hexagone, 1986.

Bélanger, Yves, and Lévesque, Michel. *René Lévesque, l'homme, la nation, la démocratie*. Quebec City: Presses de l'Université Laval, 1992.

Ferretti, Andrée, and Miron, Gaston. *Les grands textes indépendantistes 1774-1992*. Montreal: l'Hexagone, 1992.

Laforest, Guy. *Trudeau et la fin du rêve canadien*. Quebec City: Le Septentrion, 1992.

Monière, Denis. *André Laurendeau et le destin d'un peuple*. Montreal: Québec-Amérique, 1983.

Rocher, François, ed. *Bilan québécois du fédéralisme canadien*. Montreal: VLB Éditeur, 1992.

Roy, Jean-Louis. *Le choix d'un pays: Le débat constitutionnel Québec-Canada 1960-1976*. Montreal: Leméac, 1978.

Notes

1. See note 1, p. 26. *–tr.*
2. "Quebecers of old stock." *–tr.*
3. This interview was conducted before the election of the fourth French Canadian prime minister, Jean Chrétien, in 1993. *–tr.*

Biographical Notes

Robert Lahaise holds a doctorate in history from Laval University and one in literature from the University of Montreal. He is founder and editor of the *Cahiers du Québec* series at Éditions Hurtubise HMH, has written widely on Quebec culture and teaches in the history department at the University of Quebec at Montreal. His new book *La fin d'un Québec traditionnel* will be published soon by Éditions de l'Hexagone.

Jean-Paul Bernard, professor of history at the University of Quebec at Montreal, specializes in nineteenth-century history and the history and theory of the study of history. From 1979 to 1982 he was chair of the editorial board of the *Revue d'Histoire d'Amérique Française.* He is the author of *Les Rouges: Libéralisme, nationalisme et anti-cléricalisme au milieu du XIXe siècle* (Presses de l'Université du Québec, 1971) and *Les Rebellions de 1837-1838: Les Patriotes dans la mémoire collective et chez les historiens* (Boréal Express, 1983). In collaboration with the Union des Écrivains Québécois, he edited *Assemblées publiques, résolutions et déclarations de 1837-1838* (VLB Éditeur, 1988), a collection of texts produced by the two opposed movements of the time, the rebels and the loyalists.

Réal Bélanger holds a doctorate in history and is professor of history at Laval University, where he has taught since 1979. He is a specialist in political history and his research has concentrated on politicians, political parties and nationalism. He has written many books and articles and in 1990 was awarded the Prix Maxime-Raymond for his book *Wilfrid Laurier: Quand la politique devient passion* (Presses de l'Université Laval, 1987).

Pierre Trépanier holds a doctorate in history and has been professor at the University of Moncton (1976-1980) and the University of Montreal (since 1980). He is the author of *Siméon Le Sage: Un haut fonctionnaire québécois face aux défis de son temps, 1867-1909* (Bellarmin, 1979) and coeditor of the first two volumes of Lionel Groulx's correspondence (Fides, 1989 and 1993). He has published numerous articles on historiography, on the followers of the French nineteenth-century right-wing thinker Frédéric Le Play, and on right-wing movements and nationalism in French Canada. In 1988 he succeeded Philippe Sylvain in the first chair of the Société des Dix.

Robert Comeau was born in 1945 and has been a professor in the history department at the University of Quebec at Montreal since 1969. He is coauthor of *Les communistes au Québec, 1936–1956,* of *Le Parti communiste du Canada/Parti ouvrier-progressiste* and of *Histoire des maires de Montréal,* and coeditor of the "Études Québecoises" series at the publishing house VLB Éditeur.

Richard Desrosiers is a professor in the history department at the University of Quebec at Montreal specializing in the history of modern Quebec. Since 1969, he has taught in the areas of the national and political history of Quebec and the history of the labour movement. He has contributed to numerous conferences and books dealing with these areas.

Louis Balthazar holds a doctorate in political science from Harvard University, diplomas in theology and philosophy from the Jesuit Faculties of Montreal and an MA in French literature from the University of Montreal. He has been a professor in the political science department at Laval University since 1969. He was coeditor of the Department of External Affairs publication *International Perspectives* from 1974 to 1981 and a member of Quebec's Superior Council of Education from 1982 to 1986. He has published extensively on U.S. foreign policy, U.S.-Canada relations and Quebec nationalism, and his recent publications include *French Canadian Civilization* (Association for Canadian Studies in the United States, 1989); *Contemporary Quebec and the United States,* with Alfred O. Hero, Jr. (University Press of America, 1988) and *Bilan du nationalisme au Québec* (Éditions de L'Hexagone, 1986).